BREAD BAKING
Made Easy

Introduction

Ladies and gentlemen, welcome to the world of "Breads Baking Made Easy: Knead to Know." As you embark on this culinary journey through the tantalizing aroma of freshly baked goodness, allow me to extend a hearty welcome to each and every one of you.

This cookbook isn't just a compilation of recipes; it's a celebration of the artistry and simplicity that is bread baking. Inspired by a lifelong passion for the alchemy of flour, water, and yeast, I found myself compelled to unravel the secrets of this timeless craft and share them with you, my fellow kitchen adventurers.

As you flip through these pages, you'll find a treasure trove of over 100 recipes, each accompanied by visuals that aim to guide you through the enchanting process of turning basic ingredients into a symphony of flavors and textures. This isn't just about making bread; it's about understanding the nuances, embracing the simplicity, and kneading your way to the heart of a time-honored tradition.

In this book, expect to uncover the secrets behind effortless baking. From the soft whisper of a rising dough to the golden hues of a perfectly baked crust, we delve into the fundamentals that make bread not just a staple but a culinary masterpiece. Whether you're a seasoned baker or just starting to dust off your apron, there's something here for everyone.

The inspiration behind this venture lies in the simple joy of breaking bread with loved ones, the satisfaction of crafting something with your own hands, and the timeless aroma that fills a kitchen when the oven works its magic. This cookbook is an ode to those moments, a guide for both the novice and the experienced, and an invitation to savor the profound yet straightforward pleasure that is baking.

So, without further ado, preheat those ovens, dust off your rolling pins, and join me on a journey where kneading isn't just a culinary technique but a rhythmic dance with tradition. "Breads Baking Made Easy" is more than a collection of recipes; it's an invitation to knead, bake, and savor the simple magic of creating something truly extraordinary. Happy baking!

Cooking Philosophy or Approach

In the realm of flour and yeast, where the alchemy of dough transforms into the art of bread, "Breads Baking Made Easy: Knead to Know - Uncover the Secrets of Effortless Baking with Our 100+ Recipes Pictures Included" is not just a cookbook; it's a guide to a sacred ritual of sustenance.

Cooking, for me, is an intimate dance with the ingredients, a dialogue between the hands and the soul. It's a celebration of simplicity, a homage to the primal magic of turning raw elements into something nourishing and comforting.

In this cookbook, our approach is rooted in the belief that baking bread, despite its centuries-old tradition, should be an accessible and joyful experience. It's about demystifying the process, making it approachable for both the novice and the seasoned baker. We embrace the simplicity of ingredients, allowing the quality of flour, water, salt, and yeast to shine through.

The heartbeat of our philosophy is in the kneading—the rhythmic connection between hands and dough, a therapeutic communion that transforms simple ingredients into a vessel of sustenance. We champion the notion that every home should be filled with the aroma of freshly baked bread, and every individual, regardless of their baking expertise, should feel empowered to partake in this culinary tradition.

As for techniques, we've incorporated a visual journey through our recipes with included pictures. Each snapshot is a testament to the tactile nature of baking, offering a glimpse into the textures, colors, and forms that guide you on your baking odyssey. The essence lies not just in the final loaf but in the tactile experience of shaping, folding, and watching the dough evolve into a work of edible art.

Our ingredients are not exorbitant or elusive; they're the humble components that, when treated with respect and understanding, yield extraordinary results. It's a celebration of the everyday—where a handful of ingredients transforms into a loaf that nourishes both body and spirit.

So, as you embark on this journey through our cookbook, may you feel the warmth of the oven, hear the crackle of the crust, and savor the joy of breaking bread. Let the simplicity of our approach guide you, and may each knead bring you closer to the heart of baking. Happy baking, my fellow kitchen companions!

Tips for Successful Cooking

Alright, my fellow bread enthusiasts, let's talk about the bread-baking gospel we've just unleashed in "Breads Baking Made Easy: Knead to Know - Uncover the Secrets of Effortless Baking with Our 100+ Recipes Pictures Included." But before you get lost in the tantalizing aroma of fresh dough and the seduction of rising loaves, let me share a few nuggets of kitchen wisdom.

Tips for Successful Cooking:

1. Preparation is the Unsung Hero: Much like a mise en place in a bustling kitchen, having your ingredients measured, chopped, and ready before you dive into the recipe can save you from a chaotic dance with the stove. Trust me; a calm kitchen is a happy kitchen.

2. Temperature Matters: Bread, my friends, is a fickle lover. Make sure your ingredients are at room temperature, and your water is just right for yeast activation. It's a balancing act, but it's the secret to that perfect rise.

3. Patience is a Virtue, Especially with Yeast: Yeast is a living thing, and it likes a leisurely rise. Don't rush it. Give your dough the time it needs to develop those complex flavors and textures. Your patience will be rewarded with a heavenly aroma wafting through your kitchen.

4. Embrace the Imperfections: Bread is forgiving, unlike some soufflés I know. If your loaf isn't perfectly symmetrical or your scoring is a bit off, fear not. It's the quirks that make each loaf unique. Embrace the imperfect, my friends.

5. Feel the Dough: Forget the strict adherence to the clock; feel the dough under your fingers. It's a tactile experience. Learn to recognize the soft, supple touch of perfectly kneaded dough. It's a skill that comes with practice, like any culinary art.

Ingredient Selection, Preparation, and Cooking Methods:

1. Flour Power: Choose the right flour for the job. Bread flour for that robust structure, all-purpose for a more tender crumb, and experiment with whole wheat for that rustic charm. Each has its place in the bread pantheon.

2. Yeast Whispers: Use fresh, good-quality yeast. It's the conductor of the bread orchestra. If your yeast doesn't rise to the occasion, neither will your dough.

3. H2O Matters: Water is the unsung hero. The right temperature and quality can make or break your bread. Consider filtered water for the purest flavor.

4. Mix it Up: Don't be afraid to play with different flours, seeds, and grains. Bread is a canvas, and you're the artist. Mix in some flaxseeds, throw in a handful of sunflower seeds—let your imagination guide you.

5. Bake with Purpose: Preheat that oven and invest in a good baking stone or steel. A blast of high heat at the start creates that crispy crust we all crave. And don't be shy with the steam; it's the secret to a bakery-worthy crust.

Remember, my friends, bread baking is a journey. Revel in the feel of the dough, the scent of the oven, and the satisfaction of a well-baked loaf. Now, armed with these tips, let the flour fly, and may your loaves rise as high as your aspirations. Happy baking!

Kitchen Essentials

As we wrap up our exploration through the aromatic world of "Breads Baking Made Easy: Knead to Know - Uncover the Secrets of Effortless Baking with Our 100+ Recipes Pictures Included," I want to take a moment to delve into the heart of every baker's domain—the kitchen.

Kitchen Essentials:

In the culinary dance of baking, the right tools can be your greatest allies. Here's a curated list of essential kitchen tools and equipment that will waltz with you through the recipes, ensuring your journey is as seamless as the rise of a perfectly proofed dough.

1. Bread Pans:
   - Choose sturdy, non-stick bread pans for even baking and easy loaf release.

2. Mixing Bowls:
   - A set of mixing bowls in various sizes—your versatile companions for combining ingredients with grace.

3. Measuring Cups and Spoons:
   - Precision is key. Invest in quality measuring cups and spoons to accurately portion your ingredients.

4. Dough Scraper:
   - An underrated hero for manipulating dough and cleaning up your work surface effortlessly.

5. Bench Knife:
   - This multi-purpose knife is your partner in dividing dough and shaping it into perfection.

6. Kitchen Scale:
   - For the serious bakers, a kitchen scale ensures accurate measurements, a fundamental aspect of successful baking.

7. Stand Mixer or Hand Mixer:
   - A powerful ally for kneading dough and achieving the ideal consistency in your bakes.

8. Oven Thermometer:
   - Ensure your oven's honesty. An oven thermometer guarantees your creations bake at the right temperature.

Tips on How to Use These Tools Effectively:

1. Preheat Your Oven:
   - Give your oven time to reach the desired temperature before placing your creations inside.

2. Properly Measure Ingredients:
   - Level off dry ingredients in measuring cups and use the appropriate measuring tools for liquids.

3. Room Temperature Ingredients:
   - Allow ingredients like eggs and butter to come to room temperature for smoother incorporation into your recipes.

4. Follow Mixing Instructions:
   - Adhere to the specified mixing times and speeds to achieve the intended texture.

5. Properly Grease Pans:
   - Ensure an easy release by greasing your pans thoroughly or using parchment paper.

6. Let Dough Rise:
   - Patience is a virtue. Allow your dough to rise in a warm, draft-free environment for the best results.

7. Invest in Quality Tools:
   - While it's tempting to cut corners, investing in high-quality tools pays off in the long run, making your baking endeavors more enjoyable.

As you continue your baking adventures, may these essential tools and tips become the notes to your baking symphony, creating a melody of flavors that dance on your taste buds. Happy baking!

Flavor Pairing Suggestions

In the grand symphony of the culinary world, there's something truly poetic about the art of baking bread. As we wrap up our journey through "Breads Baking Made Easy: Knead to Know - Uncover the Secrets of Effortless Baking with Our 100+ Recipes," I want to leave you with a flourish—an encore that will resonate in your kitchen.

But first, let's talk about flavor pairing, that secret dance between ingredients that turns a humble loaf into a culinary masterpiece. In this cookbook, we've not only shared our tried-and-true recipes but also offered you a compass for your own culinary adventures—Flavor Pairing Suggestions.

Consider this section a backstage pass to the magic of baking. It's an invitation to the alchemical process where flour, water, and yeast transcend their individual roles and become a harmonious ensemble. Here, we provide ideas for complementary flavors, guiding you through the symphony of tastes that work seamlessly together.

Ever wondered about the aromatic embrace of rosemary and olive oil in a rustic Italian bread? Or perhaps the sweet dance of honey and oats in a morning loaf? These suggestions are not just about following a recipe; they're an ode to experimentation, an encouragement to let your taste buds lead the way.

So, as you venture into the realm of your own bread-making creations, let the Flavor Pairing Suggestions be your sheet music. Feel free to improvise, compose, and let your kitchen become the stage for your culinary concerto.

And now, as our final act, I'd like to ask for a standing ovation of sorts. Reviews, my fellow bakers, are the applause that resonates in the hearts of every cookbook creator. If you've found the rhythm in our recipes, the harmony in our suggestions, I kindly ask you to share your thoughts. Head back to your app or the online marketplace where you discovered this baking journey, find that review button, and let us know your rating and a short sentence about your experience.

Reviews are the yeast that help our small publishing bakery rise. They are the encouragement that fuels us to continue sharing the joy of bread-making. We read each one with the same excitement as a baker waiting for that perfect golden crust to emerge from the oven.

Your support means the world to us. Thank you for allowing our recipes to grace your kitchen, and may your future bread-making endeavors be filled with the delightful aroma of success. Happy baking!

INDEX

Chapter 1: Classic Artisan Breads

2 baguettes

150 calories per serving

120 minutes

Crusty French Baguette

Ingredients:

- 500g bread flour
- 10g salt
- 10g sugar
- 7g active dry yeast
- 350ml lukewarm water

Fun Fact

The French baguette was first created in the 18th century and was initially called pain viennois or Viennese bread. It later evolved into the iconic baguette we know today.

Transport yourself to a quaint French bakery with this Crusty French Baguette. Its golden, crisp crust and soft, airy interior are a testament to the art of French bread-making. A symbol of Gallic culinary excellence, this baguette will elevate any meal.

Directions

1. In a large bowl, combine the flour, salt, and sugar.
2. In a separate bowl, mix the yeast with lukewarm water and let it sit for 5 minutes.
3. Add the yeast mixture to the dry ingredients and knead until a smooth dough forms.
4. Cover and let it rise for 1 hour.
5. Preheat your oven to 450°F (230°C).
6. Shape the dough into two baguettes and let them rise for another 30 minutes.
7. Score the tops and bake for 25-30 minutes.
8. Enjoy fresh or with your favorite spread.

4 servings

200 calories per serving

180 minutes

Italian Ciabatta

Ingredients:

- 500g bread flour
- 10g salt
- 7g active dry yeast
- 350ml lukewarm water

Dive into the rustic charm of Italian cuisine with this Ciabatta bread. Its crunchy crust and soft, hole-ridden interior are perfect for dipping in olive oil or making sandwiches. Originally from Verona, this bread has gained worldwide popularity.

Directions

1. In a bowl, mix the flour and salt.
2. In another bowl, dissolve the yeast in lukewarm water.
3. Combine the wet and dry ingredients and knead for 10 minutes.
4. Let the dough rise for 1 hour.
5. Preheat the oven to 450°F (230°C).
6. Shape the dough into rectangles and let it rest for 15 minutes.
7. Bake for 20-25 minutes.
8. Savor the taste of Italy.

Fun Fact

Ciabatta means slipper bread in Italian, named for its elongated, flat shape resembling an old-style slipper.

1 boule

160 calories per serving

1440 minutes

Sourdough Boule

Ingredients:

- 500g bread flour
- 10g salt
- 100g active sourdough starter
- 350ml lukewarm water

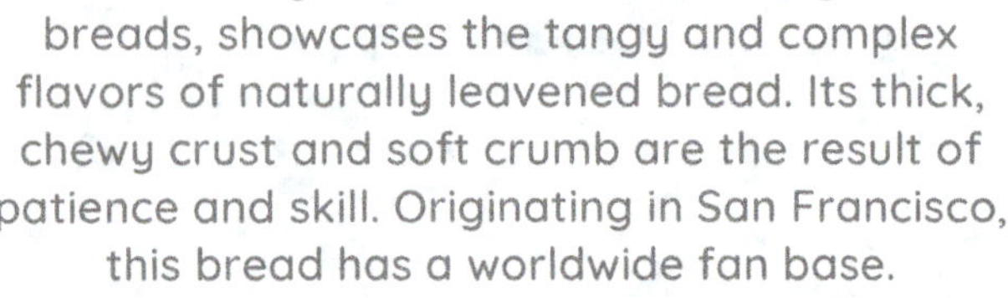

The Sourdough Boule, a classic among artisan breads, showcases the tangy and complex flavors of naturally leavened bread. Its thick, chewy crust and soft crumb are the result of patience and skill. Originating in San Francisco, this bread has a worldwide fan base.

Directions

1. Mix flour and salt in a bowl.
2. Add sourdough starter and water.
3. Knead the dough until it's smooth.
4. Let it rise for 12 hours.
5. Preheat the oven to 450°F (230°C).
6. Shape the dough into a boule and score the top.
7. Bake for 35-40 minutes.
8. Taste the San Francisco tradition.

Fun Fact

Sourdough bread is made using a natural fermentation process that involves wild yeast and lactic acid bacteria.

1 loaf

120 calories per serving

180 minutes

Rye Caraway Loaf

The Rye Caraway Loaf is a hearty and wholesome choice, offering a rich, earthy flavor with a hint of caraway spice. Originating in Germany, it's a staple at family gatherings and holidays. Enjoy it with savory spreads or in sandwiches.

Ingredients:

- 300g rye flour
- 200g bread flour
- 10g salt
- 7g active dry yeast
- 10g caraway seeds
- 350ml lukewarm water

Directions

1. Mix rye and bread flours, salt, and caraway seeds.
2. Dissolve yeast in lukewarm water and add to the dry ingredients.
3. Knead until smooth.
4. Let it rise for 1 hour.
5. Preheat the oven to 400°F (200°C).
6. Shape the dough into a loaf and let it rest.
7. Bake for 40-45 minutes.
8. Celebrate the taste of Germany.

Fun Fact

Rye bread is known for its health benefits, including being a good source of fiber and essential nutrients.

1 loaf

110 calories per serving

240 minutes

Whole Wheat Country Bread

Ingredients:

- 400g whole wheat flour
- 100g bread flour
- 10g salt
- 7g active dry yeast
- 350ml lukewarm water

The Whole Wheat Country Bread embodies simplicity and health. Made with whole wheat flour, it has a rustic appeal and a nutty flavor. Enjoy it with your favorite spreads or as a companion to hearty soups.

Directions

1. Combine whole wheat and bread flours with salt.
2. Dissolve yeast in lukewarm water and add to the dry ingredients.
3. Knead until smooth.
4. Let it rise for 2 hours.
5. Preheat the oven to 400°F (200°C).
6. Shape the dough into a loaf and let it rest.
7. Bake for 35-40 minutes.
8. Enjoy rustic goodness.

Fun Fact

Whole wheat bread is an excellent source of dietary fiber and provides a range of essential nutrients.

1 loaf

150 calories per serving

180 minutes

Challah Bread

Normal

Challah Bread is a braided, slightly sweet bread that's a favorite for Jewish holidays and celebrations. It symbolizes unity and tradition, making it a cherished recipe.

Ingredients:

- 500g bread flour
- 10g salt
- 7g active dry yeast
- 3 eggs
- 100g sugar
- 150ml lukewarm water
- 50ml vegetable oil

Directions

1. Combine flour and salt in a bowl.
2. In another bowl, whisk the yeast with water and sugar.
3. Add eggs and oil to the yeast mixture.
4. Mix wet and dry ingredients and knead.
5. Let it rise for 1.5 hours.
6. Preheat the oven to 350°F (175°C).
7. Braid the dough and let it rise for 30 minutes.
8. Bake for 30-35 minutes.
9. Celebrate with this meaningful bread.

Fun Fact

Challah bread is often braided with three, four, or six strands, each having its unique symbolic meaning in Jewish traditions.

1 round
loaf

120
calories
per
serving

150
minutes

Portuguese
Cornbread

Ingredients:

- 250g cornmeal
- 250g bread flour
- 10g salt
- 7g active dry yeast
- 300ml lukewarm water

Portuguese Cornbread, known as Broa, is a rustic, hearty bread made with cornmeal and wheat flour. It has a dense, moist crumb and is a staple in Portuguese cuisine.

Directions

1. Mix cornmeal, flour, and salt in a bowl.
2. Dissolve yeast in lukewarm water.
3. Combine wet and dry ingredients and knead.
4. Let it rise for 1 hour.
5. Preheat the oven to 375°F (190°C).
6. Shape the dough into a round loaf.
7. Bake for 40-45 minutes.
8. Experience the flavors of Portugal.

Fun Fact

Broa is often enjoyed with traditional Portuguese dishes, such as bacalhau (salted codfish) and caldo verde (green soup).

1
flatbread

200
calories
per
serving

120
minutes

Focaccia with Herbs and Olives

Ingredients:

- 500g bread flour
- 10g salt
- 7g active dry yeast
- 2 tbsp fresh rosemary
- 100g pitted olives
- 350ml lukewarm water
- 50ml olive oil

Focaccia with Herbs and Olives is an Italian flatbread, known for its dimpled surface, rosemary, olives, and olive oil. It's a delightful accompaniment to any Mediterranean meal.

Directions

1. Combine flour and salt in a bowl.
2. In a separate bowl, dissolve yeast in water.
3. Mix wet and dry ingredients and knead.
4. Let it rise for 1 hour.
5. Preheat the oven to 450°F (230°C).
6. Shape the dough into a flatbread.
7. Dimple the surface and top with rosemary and olives.
8. Drizzle with olive oil.
9. Bake for 20-25 minutes.
10. Embrace Mediterranean flavors.

Fun Fact

Focaccia is believed to have originated in ancient Etruria, in what is now Italy. It has a long history dating back to the Roman Empire.

1 loaf

130 calories per serving

240 minutes

Swedish Limpa Bread

Ingredients:

- 250g rye flour
- 250g bread flour
- 10g salt
- 7g active dry yeast
- 2 tsp anise seeds
- Zest of 1 orange
- 350ml lukewarm water

Swedish Limpa Bread is a sweet and slightly spicy rye bread. It's a popular choice during the holiday season in Sweden, with flavors of anise and orange zest.

Directions

1. Mix rye and bread flours, salt, anise seeds, and orange zest in a bowl.
2. Dissolve yeast in lukewarm water and add to the dry ingredients.
3. Knead until smooth.
4. Let it rise for 2 hours.
5. Preheat the oven to 375°F (190°C).
6. Shape the dough into a loaf.
7. Bake for 35-40 minutes.
8. Celebrate Swedish traditions.

Fun Fact

Limpa bread is a Swedish holiday tradition, often enjoyed during Christmas and other festive occasions.

1 loaf

110 calories per serving

1440 minutes

Dutch Oven No-Knead Bread

Dutch Oven No-Knead Bread is a simple yet flavorful artisan bread. The dough is left to ferment for a long time, resulting in a chewy interior and a crispy crust.

Ingredients:

- 500g bread flour
- 10g salt
- 2g active dry yeast
- 350ml lukewarm water

Directions

1. Mix flour and salt in a bowl.
2. Dissolve yeast in lukewarm water and add to the dry ingredients.
3. Mix until just combined.
4. Cover and let it rise for 12-18 hours.
5. Preheat the oven to 450°F (230°C) with a Dutch oven inside.
6. Transfer the dough into the hot Dutch oven and cover with the lid.
7. Bake for 30 minutes with the lid on and 15-20 minutes with the lid off.
8. Enjoy the simplicity of no-knead bread.

Fun Fact

No-knead bread is a perfect choice for those who want to enjoy homemade artisan bread with minimal effort.

Chapter 2: Flavors of the World

4 naans

150 calories per serving

120 minutes

Indian Naan Bread

Ingredients:

- 500g all-purpose flour
- 10g salt
- 7g active dry yeast
- 150ml yogurt
- 50ml vegetable oil
- 150ml lukewarm water

Indian Naan Bread is a soft, leavened flatbread that's a staple in Indian cuisine. It's perfect for scooping up curries or using as a wrap for kebabs.

Directions

1. Mix flour and salt in a bowl.
2. In another bowl, dissolve yeast in lukewarm water and add yogurt and oil.
3. Combine wet and dry ingredients and knead.
4. Let it rise for 1 hour.
5. Preheat the oven to its highest setting (typically around 500°F or 260°C).
6. Divide the dough into 4 portions and shape them into teardrop or oval naans.
7. Bake on a preheated baking stone or sheet for 2-3 minutes, until they puff up and brown.
8. Enjoy the flavors of India.

Fun Fact

Naan bread can be traced back to the Indian subcontinent, and it's a popular accompaniment to many Indian dishes, particularly in North India.

4
bolillos

180
calories
per
serving

150
minutes

Mexican Bolillos

Ingredients:

- 500g bread flour
- 10g salt
- 7g active dry yeast
- 350ml lukewarm water

Bolillos are crusty, elongated rolls that are a common sight in Mexican bakeries. They're great for making tortas (Mexican sandwiches) or enjoying with butter and jam.

Directions

1. Mix flour and salt in a bowl.
2. Dissolve yeast in lukewarm water.
3. Knead the dough until smooth.
4. Let it rise for 1 hour.
5. Preheat the oven to 400°F (200°C).
6. Shape the dough into 4 bolillos.
7. Bake for 20-25 minutes.
8. Savor the taste of Mexico.

Fun Fact

Bolillos are a key component of Mexican street food and are often used for making sandwiches like tortas.

8 pitas

130 calories per serving

120 minutes

Greek Pita Bread

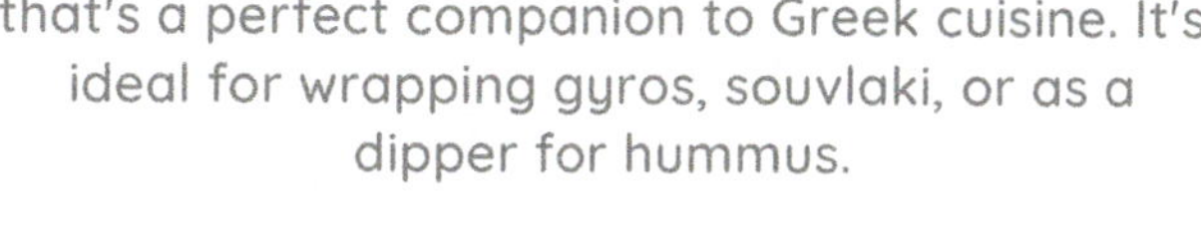

Greek Pita Bread is a soft, round flatbread that's a perfect companion to Greek cuisine. It's ideal for wrapping gyros, souvlaki, or as a dipper for hummus.

Ingredients:

- 500g bread flour
- 10g salt
- 7g active dry yeast
- 350ml lukewarm water

Directions

1. Mix flour and salt in a bowl.
2. Dissolve yeast in lukewarm water.
3. Knead the dough until smooth.
4. Let it rise for 1 hour.
5. Preheat the oven to 500°F (260°C) with a baking stone or sheet inside.
6. Divide the dough into 8 portions and roll them into thin circles.
7. Place on the preheated baking surface and bake for 2-3 minutes, until they puff up.
8. Enjoy a taste of Greece.

Fun Fact

Pita bread is a versatile staple in Mediterranean and Middle Eastern cuisines, often used for both sweet and savory dishes.

2 pides

200 calories per serving

180 minutes

Turkish Pide

Ingredients:

- 500g bread flour
- 10g salt
- 7g active dry yeast
- 350ml lukewarm water
- 50ml olive oil

Turkish Pide is an elongated flatbread, often topped with various ingredients like ground meat, vegetables, and herbs. It's a popular dish in Turkey and beyond.

Directions

1. Mix flour and salt in a bowl.
2. Dissolve yeast in lukewarm water and add olive oil.
3. Knead the dough until smooth.
4. Let it rise for 1.5 hours.
5. Preheat the oven to 450°F (230°C).
6. Divide the dough into 2 portions and shape them into elongated ovals.
7. Add your choice of toppings.
8. Bake for 15-20 minutes.
9. Relish the flavors of Turkey.

Fun Fact

Pide has been a part of Turkish cuisine for centuries and is enjoyed in various forms across the Middle East and the Balkans.

 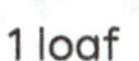  

1 loaf

160 calories per serving

240 minutes

Scandinavian Cardamom Bread

Scandinavian Cardamom Bread, also known as Pulla, is a sweet, aromatic bread infused with cardamom spice. It's a delightful treat often enjoyed with coffee or tea.

Ingredients:

- 500g bread flour
- 10g salt
- 7g active dry yeast
- 100g sugar
- 10g ground cardamom
- 300ml lukewarm milk
- 100g unsalted butter

Directions

1. Mix flour, salt, sugar, and ground cardamom in a bowl.
2. Dissolve yeast in lukewarm milk.
3. Add softened butter and combine with dry ingredients.
4. Knead the dough until smooth.
5. Let it rise for 2 hours.
6. Preheat the oven to 375°F (190°C).
7. Shape the dough into a loaf.
8. Bake for 35-40 minutes.
9. Enjoy a taste of Scandinavia.

Fun Fact

Cardamom is a key spice in Scandinavian baking and adds a unique and fragrant flavor to the bread.

1 loaf

140 calories per serving

180 minutes

Japanese Milk Bread

Ingredients:

- 500g bread flour
- 10g salt
- 7g active dry yeast
- 50g sugar
- 50g unsalted butter
- 250ml warm milk

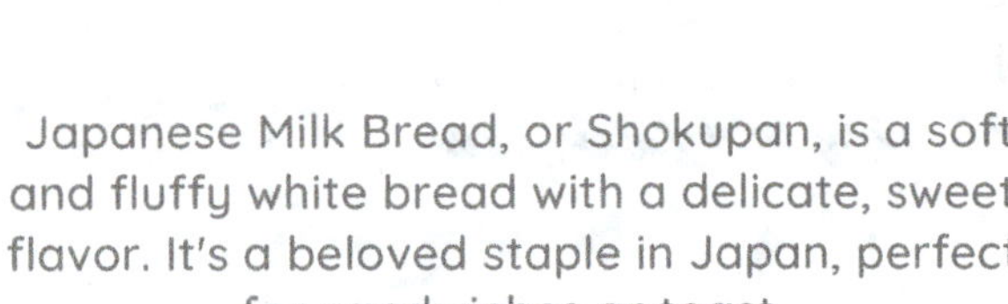

Japanese Milk Bread, or Shokupan, is a soft and fluffy white bread with a delicate, sweet flavor. It's a beloved staple in Japan, perfect for sandwiches or toast.

Directions

1. Mix flour and salt in a bowl.
2. In another bowl, dissolve yeast in warm milk and add sugar and softened butter.
3. Combine wet and dry ingredients and knead until smooth.
4. Let it rise for 1.5 hours.
5. Preheat the oven to 350°F (175°C).
6. Shape the dough into a loaf.
7. Bake for 25-30 minutes.
8. Experience the fluffiness of Japanese bread.

Fun Fact

Japanese Milk Bread is a popular base for katsu sandwiches, a classic Japanese sandwich featuring breaded and fried meat or vegetables.

1 loaf

110 calories per serving

75 minutes

Irish Soda Bread

Irish Soda Bread is a traditional quick bread from Ireland, made with just a few simple ingredients. It has a crusty exterior and a dense, hearty interior.

Ingredients:

- 450g all-purpose flour
- 1 tsp salt
- 1 tsp baking soda
- 375ml buttermilk

Directions

1. Preheat the oven to 425°F (220°C).
2. In a large bowl, mix flour, salt, and baking soda.
3. Make a well in the center and pour in buttermilk.
4. Stir until the dough comes together.
5. Shape the dough into a round loaf.
6. Place on a baking sheet and score a deep cross on top.
7. Bake for 15 minutes at 425°F, then reduce the oven to 400°F (200°C) and bake for an additional 15-20 minutes.
8. Enjoy a taste of Ireland.

Fun Fact

The cross on top of Irish Soda Bread is believed to ward off evil and protect the household.

1 round
loaf

150
calories
per
serving

180
minutes

Moroccan Khobz

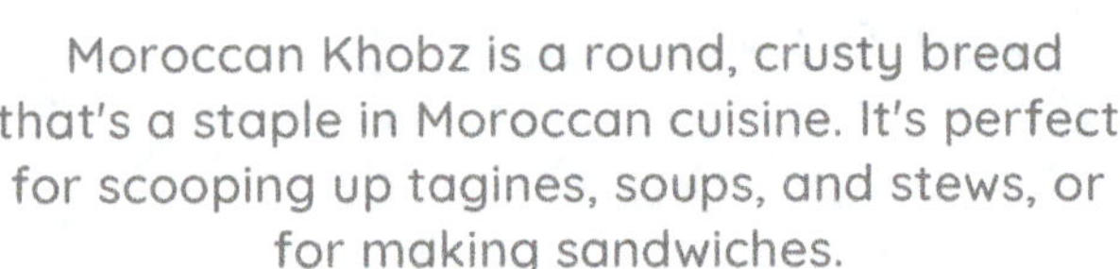

Ingredients:

- 500g bread flour
- 10g salt
- 7g active dry yeast
- 350ml lukewarm water

Moroccan Khobz is a round, crusty bread that's a staple in Moroccan cuisine. It's perfect for scooping up tagines, soups, and stews, or for making sandwiches.

Directions

1. Mix flour and salt in a bowl.
2. Dissolve yeast in lukewarm water.
3. Knead the dough until smooth.
4. Let it rise for 2 hours.
5. Preheat the oven to 425°F (220°C).
6. Shape the dough into a round loaf.
7. Bake for 25-30 minutes.
8. Savor the flavors of Morocco.

Fun Fact

Khobz is often served as a staple bread at Moroccan meals and is an essential part of Moroccan culture.

12 empana das

200 calories per serving

120 minutes

Argentinean Empanadas

Ingredients:

- 400g all-purpose flour
- 1 tsp salt
- 200g unsalted butter
- 100ml cold water

Argentinean Empanadas are savory hand pies filled with various ingredients, popular throughout South America. They can be filled with meat, cheese, vegetables, or sweet fillings.

Directions

1. In a bowl, mix flour and salt.
2. Add cold, diced butter and combine until crumbly.
3. Gradually add cold water and knead into a dough.
4. Let it rest for 30 minutes in the refrigerator.
5. Roll out the dough and cut circles.
6. Fill with your choice of ingredients.
7. Fold the dough over and seal.
8. Bake at 375°F (190°C) for 20-25 minutes.
9. Enjoy a taste of Argentina.

Fun Fact

Empanadas are popular street food in Argentina, and they come in various styles and fillings.

1 loaf

130 calories per serving

240 minutes

Russian Black Bread

Russian Black Bread, often known as Borodinsky bread, is a dark and hearty rye bread with a rich, complex flavor. It's a classic in Russian cuisine.

Ingredients:

- 250g rye flour
- 250g bread flour
- 10g salt
- 10g sugar
- 7g active dry yeast
- 50ml molasses
- 350ml lukewarm water

Directions

1. Mix rye and bread flours, salt, sugar, and yeast in a bowl.
2. Dissolve molasses in lukewarm water and add to dry ingredients.
3. Knead until smooth.
4. Let it rise for 2 hours.
5. Preheat the oven to 375°F (190°C).
6. Shape the dough into a loaf.
7. Bake for 35-40 minutes.
8. Savor the depth of Russian flavors.

Fun Fact

Russian Black Bread is a traditional bread with a history dating back to the 19th century. It's often associated with Russian folklore and culture.

Chapter 3:
Sweet and Savory Rolls

 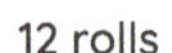  

12 rolls

300 calories per serving

180 minutes

Cinnamon Rolls with Cream Cheese Frosting

Cinnamon Rolls with Cream Cheese Frosting are a sweet indulgence. Soft, cinnamon-spiced dough swirled with a gooey filling and topped with luscious cream cheese frosting. Perfect for breakfast or dessert.

Ingredients:

- 500g all-purpose flour
- 10g salt
- 7g active dry yeast
- 250ml warm milk
- 50g unsalted butter
- 50g granulated sugar
- 1 egg
- For the filling: 100g brown sugar, 2 tbsp ground cinnamon
- For the frosting: 150g cream cheese, 50g unsalted butter, 150g powdered sugar, 1 tsp vanilla extract

Directions

1. In a bowl, mix flour and salt.
2. In another bowl, dissolve yeast in warm milk, then add butter, sugar, and egg.
3. Combine wet and dry ingredients to form a dough.
4. Let it rise for 1.5 hours.
5. Roll out the dough into a rectangle.
6. Spread the filling over the dough.
7. Roll up the dough and cut into 12 rolls.
8. Place the rolls in a baking dish.
9. Bake at 375°F (190°C) for 25-30 minutes.
10. While baking, make the cream cheese frosting.
11. Frost the rolls while warm.
12. Enjoy this sweet treat.

Fun Fact

Cinnamon rolls have been a beloved baked good for generations, with various regional variations and cultural adaptations.

12 rolls

150 calories per serving

150 minutes

Garlic Parmesan Dinner Rolls

Garlic Parmesan Dinner Rolls are a savory delight. Soft and fluffy rolls infused with garlic and topped with a sprinkle of Parmesan cheese. A perfect side dish for any meal.

Ingredients:

- 500g all-purpose flour
- 10g salt
- 7g active dry yeast
- 250ml warm milk
- 50g unsalted butter
- 2 cloves garlic, minced
- 50g grated Parmesan cheese

Directions

1. In a bowl, mix flour and salt.
2. In another bowl, dissolve yeast in warm milk, then add butter and minced garlic.
3. Combine wet and dry ingredients to form a dough.
4. Let it rise for 1 hour.
5. Roll out the dough and cut into 12 rolls.
6. Place the rolls in a baking dish.
7. Sprinkle Parmesan cheese on top.
8. Bake at 375°F (190°C) for 20-25 minutes.
9. Savor the garlic and Parmesan goodness.

Fun Fact

Garlic Parmesan Dinner Rolls are a popular side dish in many Italian and American meals, especially at family gatherings.

12 rolls

180 calories per serving

180 minutes

Hawaiian Sweet Rolls

Ingredients:

- 500g bread flour
- 10g salt
- 7g active dry yeast
- 250ml warm milk
- 50g unsalted butter
- 50g sugar
- 125ml pineapple juice
- 1 egg

Hawaiian Sweet Rolls are soft and sweet, with a hint of pineapple flavor. They're perfect for making sliders, but also great on their own as a sweet and fluffy roll.

Directions

1. Mix flour and salt in a bowl.
2. In another bowl, dissolve yeast in warm milk, then add butter, sugar, egg, and pineapple juice.
3. Combine wet and dry ingredients to form a dough.
4. Let it rise for 1.5 hours.
5. Roll out the dough and cut into 12 rolls.
6. Place the rolls in a baking dish.
7. Bake at 375°F (190°C) for 20-25 minutes.
8. Enjoy a taste of the tropics.

Fun Fact

Hawaiian Sweet Rolls are a popular bread choice in Hawaii and have gained popularity in other parts of the world.

6
servings

220
calories
per
serving

150
minutes

Pretzel Bites with Cheese Sauce

Pretzel Bites with Cheese Sauce are a savory and addictive snack. Soft and chewy pretzel bites, served with a creamy cheese sauce for dipping. Perfect for parties and gatherings.

Ingredients:

- 500g bread flour
- 10g salt
- 7g active dry yeast
- 250ml warm water
- 50g granulated sugar
- 60g baking soda
- For the cheese sauce: 200g cheddar cheese, 100ml milk, 1 tsp mustard, 1/2 tsp paprika

Directions

1. Mix flour and salt in a bowl.
2. In another bowl, dissolve yeast in warm water and add sugar.
3. Combine wet and dry ingredients to form a dough.
4. Let it rise for 1 hour.
5. Roll out the dough and cut into bite-sized pieces.
6. Boil water with baking soda and briefly dip each piece.
7. Place on a baking sheet and bake at 425°F (220°C) for 15-20 minutes.
8. While baking, make the cheese sauce.
9. Serve the pretzel bites with the cheese sauce.
10. Enjoy this delicious snack.

Fun Fact

Pretzel bites are a popular snack in many parts of the world and are commonly found at sports events and festivals.

12 rolls

160 calories per serving

180 minutes

Spinach and Feta Stuffed Rolls

Spinach and Feta Stuffed Rolls are a delightful combination of flavors. Soft rolls filled with spinach and feta cheese, creating a savory, cheesy, and veggie-packed treat.

Ingredients:

- 500g all-purpose flour
- 10g salt
- 7g active dry yeast
- 250ml warm milk
- 50g unsalted butter
- 200g frozen spinach, thawed and squeezed dry
- 200g feta cheese, crumbled
- 2 cloves garlic, minced

Directions

1. Mix flour and salt in a bowl.
2. In another bowl, dissolve yeast in warm milk, then add butter.
3. Combine wet and dry ingredients to form a dough.
4. Let it rise for 1.5 hours.
5. Roll out the dough and cut into 12 squares.
6. Place spinach, feta, and minced garlic on each square.
7. Fold the dough to enclose the filling and shape into rolls.
8. Place the rolls in a baking dish.
9. Bake at 375°F (190°C) for 20-25 minutes.
10. Enjoy these savory stuffed rolls.

Fun Fact

Spinach and Feta Stuffed Rolls are a great appetizer or side dish, combining the flavors of Mediterranean cuisine with soft, homemade rolls.

12 muffins

180 calories per serving

30 minutes

Jalapeño Cheddar Cornbread Muffins

Ingredients:

- 200g cornmeal
- 100g all-purpose flour
- 10g baking powder
- 5g salt
- 200ml milk
- 2 eggs
- 60g melted butter
- 2 jalapeños, finely chopped
- 150g cheddar cheese, shredded

Fun Fact

Jalapeño Cheddar Cornbread Muffins are a perfect accompaniment to chili, barbecue, or any Southwestern-inspired meal.

Jalapeño Cheddar Cornbread Muffins are a spicy and cheesy delight. Moist cornbread muffins with a kick of jalapeño heat and the savory goodness of cheddar cheese.

Directions

1. Preheat the oven to 400°F (200°C) and prepare a muffin tin.
2. In a bowl, mix cornmeal, flour, baking powder, and salt.
3. In another bowl, whisk together milk, eggs, and melted butter.
4. Combine wet and dry ingredients.
5. Fold in chopped jalapeños and shredded cheddar.
6. Spoon the batter into the muffin tin.
7. Bake for 15-20 minutes, until golden.
8. Enjoy the spicy and cheesy goodness.

12 rolls

150 calories per serving

180 minutes

Jalapeño Cheddar Cornbread Muffins

Pumpkin Dinner Rolls are a delightful fall treat. Soft and tender dinner rolls with the subtle sweetness and earthy flavor of pumpkin. Perfect for holiday meals.

Ingredients:

- 500g bread flour
- 10g salt
- 7g active dry yeast
- 250ml warm milk
- 100g canned pumpkin puree
- 50g sugar
- 50g unsalted butter

Directions

1. Mix flour and salt in a bowl.
2. In another bowl, dissolve yeast in warm milk, then add pumpkin puree, sugar, and butter.
3. Combine wet and dry ingredients to form a dough.
4. Let it rise for 1.5 hours.
5. Roll out the dough and cut into 12 rolls.
6. Place the rolls in a baking dish.
7. Bake at 375°F (190°C) for 20-25 minutes.
8. Enjoy the flavors of fall.

Fun Fact

Pumpkin Dinner Rolls are a popular addition to Thanksgiving and other holiday feasts, bringing a touch of seasonal warmth to the table.

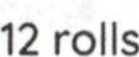

12 rolls

160 calories per serving

180 minutes

Lemon Poppy Seed Rolls

Ingredients:

- 500g all-purpose flour
- 10g salt
- 7g active dry yeast
- 250ml warm milk
- 50g sugar
- Zest of 2 lemons
- Juice of 1 lemon
- 1 tbsp poppy seeds

Lemon Poppy Seed Rolls are a burst of citrusy goodness. Soft and fluffy rolls infused with zesty lemon and speckled with poppy seeds. A delightful and refreshing treat.

Directions

1. Mix flour and salt in a bowl.
2. In another bowl, dissolve yeast in warm milk, then add sugar, lemon zest, lemon juice, and poppy seeds.
3. Combine wet and dry ingredients to form a dough.
4. Let it rise for 1.5 hours.
5. Roll out the dough and cut into 12 rolls.
6. Place the rolls in a baking dish.
7. Bake at 375°F (190°C) for 20-25 minutes.
8. Enjoy the bright and zesty flavors.

Fun Fact

Lemon Poppy Seed Rolls are a perfect addition to brunch or tea time, bringing a burst of citrus and a delightful crunch.

 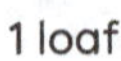  

1 loaf

220 calories per serving

180 minutes

Bacon and Chive Pull-Apart Bread

Ingredients:

- 500g bread flour
- 10g salt
- 7g active dry yeast
- 250ml warm milk
- 50g unsalted butter
- 100g cooked bacon, crumbled
- 2 tbsp fresh chives, chopped
- 150g cheddar cheese, shredded

Fun Fact

Pull-apart bread is a fun and shareable treat that can be customized with various fillings, from savory to sweet.

Bacon and Chive Pull-Apart Bread is a savory and irresistible treat. Soft bread filled with crispy bacon, chives, and cheese, perfect for tearing apart and sharing.

Directions

1. Mix flour and salt in a bowl.
2. In another bowl, dissolve yeast in warm milk, then add butter.
3. Combine wet and dry ingredients to form a dough.
4. Let it rise for 1.5 hours.
5. Roll out the dough into a rectangle.
6. Sprinkle bacon, chives, and shredded cheddar over the dough.
7. Cut the dough into strips and stack them in a loaf pan.
8. Bake at 375°F (190°C) for 30-35 minutes.
9. Enjoy the savory goodness.

12 rolls

170 calories per serving

180 minutes

Cranberry Walnut Rolls

Ingredients:

- 500g all-purpose flour
- 10g salt
- 7g active dry yeast
- 250ml warm milk
- 50g sugar
- 50g unsalted butter
- 100g dried cranberries
- 100g toasted walnuts, chopped

Cranberry Walnut Rolls are a combination of sweet and nutty flavors. Soft rolls studded with dried cranberries and toasted walnuts, making them perfect for a holiday spread.

Directions

1. Mix flour and salt in a bowl.
2. In another bowl, dissolve yeast in warm milk, then add sugar and butter.
3. Combine wet and dry ingredients to form a dough.
4. Let it rise for 1.5 hours.
5. Fold in dried cranberries and chopped toasted walnuts.
6. Roll out the dough and cut into 12 rolls.
7. Place the rolls in a baking dish.
8. Bake at 375°F (190°C) for 20-25 minutes.
9. Enjoy the sweet and nutty combination.

Fun Fact

Cranberry Walnut Rolls are a delightful addition to holiday meals and are often enjoyed as part of festive spreads.

Chapter 4: Gluten-Free Creations

 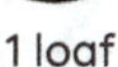  

1 loaf

150 calories per serving

180 minutes

Gluten-Free Artisan Bread

Ingredients:

- 500g gluten-free all-purpose flour
- 10g salt
- 7g active dry yeast
- 250ml warm water
- 50ml olive oil

Gluten-Free Artisan Bread is a wonderful alternative for those with gluten sensitivity. It offers the texture and flavor of traditional artisan bread without gluten.

Directions

1. Mix gluten-free flour and salt in a bowl.
2. In another bowl, dissolve yeast in warm water and add olive oil.
3. Combine wet and dry ingredients to form a dough.
4. Let it rise for 1.5 hours.
5. Preheat the oven to 400°F (200°C).
6. Shape the dough into a loaf.
7. Bake for 25-30 minutes.
8. Enjoy gluten-free goodness.

Fun Fact

Gluten-Free Artisan Bread allows individuals with gluten sensitivity to enjoy the taste and texture of traditional artisan bread.

1
focaccia

160
calories
per
serving

150
minutes

Rosemary and Olive Focaccia (Gluten-Free)

Rosemary and Olive Focaccia is a gluten-free take on the classic Italian bread. It's fragrant with rosemary and adorned with olives for a burst of Mediterranean flavors.

Ingredients:

- 500g gluten-free all-purpose flour
- 10g salt
- 7g active dry yeast
- 250ml warm water
- 50ml olive oil
- Fresh rosemary
- Pitted olives

Directions

1. Mix gluten-free flour and salt in a bowl.
2. In another bowl, dissolve yeast in warm water and add olive oil.
3. Combine wet and dry ingredients to form a dough.
4. Let it rise for 1 hour.
5. Preheat the oven to 400°F (200°C).
6. Shape the dough into a focaccia shape.
7. Press rosemary and olives into the dough.
8. Bake for 20-25 minutes.
9. Savor the Mediterranean flavors.

Fun Fact

Focaccia is a popular Italian flatbread known for its versatility in flavor and toppings.

6 bagels

220 calories per serving

120 minutes

Almond Flour Bagels (Gluten-Free)

Almond Flour Bagels are a gluten-free twist on a breakfast classic. These bagels are made with almond flour, resulting in a nutty and satisfying texture.

Ingredients:

- 300g almond flour
- 5g baking powder
- 5g salt
- 3 eggs
- 60ml olive oil
- 100ml warm water

Directions

1. Preheat the oven to 350°F (175°C) and prepare a baking sheet.
2. In a bowl, mix almond flour, baking powder, and salt.
3. In another bowl, whisk eggs, olive oil, and warm water.
4. Combine wet and dry ingredients to form a dough.
5. Divide the dough into 6 portions and shape them into bagels.
6. Place the bagels on the baking sheet.
7. Bake for 20-25 minutes.
8. Enjoy gluten-free bagels.

Fun Fact

Almond Flour Bagels offer a grain-free and gluten-free alternative to traditional bagels, perfect for those with dietary restrictions.

4 injera

120 calories per serving

120 minutes

Teff Injera (Gluten-Free)

Ingredients:

- 250g teff flour
- 5g salt
- 375ml warm water

Teff Injera is a traditional Ethiopian flatbread made with teff flour. It's naturally gluten-free and has a unique, slightly sour flavor. Perfect for scooping up stews and curries.

Directions

1. In a bowl, mix teff flour and salt.
2. Gradually add warm water to the flour and stir to form a batter.
3. Cover the bowl and let the batter ferment for 8-12 hours or overnight.
4. Preheat a non-stick pan or injera grill.
5. Pour a ladle of the batter onto the hot surface and spread it in a circular motion to form a thin pancake.
6. Cook until the surface is dry and the edges lift.
7. Injera is ready when the top is covered with small holes.
8. Serve with your favorite Ethiopian dishes.

Fun Fact

Teff Injera is a staple in Ethiopian cuisine and serves as both a food and a utensil, allowing you to scoop up flavorful stews and dishes.

1 loaf

140 calories per serving

75 minutes

Gluten-Free Irish Soda Bread

Gluten-Free Irish Soda Bread offers a gluten-free version of the classic Irish quick bread. It's made with a mix of gluten-free flours and has a hearty, crumbly texture.

Ingredients:

- 300g gluten-free all-purpose flour
- 200g gluten-free oat flour
- 10g salt
- 5g baking soda
- 300ml buttermilk

Directions

1. Preheat the oven to 425°F (220°C).
2. In a bowl, mix gluten-free flours, salt, and baking soda.
3. Make a well in the center and pour in buttermilk.
4. Stir until the dough comes together.
5. Shape the dough into a round loaf.
6. Place on a baking sheet and score a deep cross on top.
7. Bake for 15 minutes at 425°F, then reduce the oven to 400°F (200°C) and bake for an additional 20-25 minutes.
8. Enjoy the gluten-free twist on a traditional Irish favorite.

Fun Fact

Irish Soda Bread is a classic and simple bread that's quick to make and doesn't require yeast. It's often enjoyed with butter and jam.

1 loaf

190 calories per serving

90 minutes

Banana Nut Bread (Gluten-Free)

Banana Nut Bread (Gluten-Free) is a moist and flavorful gluten-free version of the classic banana bread. Packed with the goodness of ripe bananas and crunchy nuts.

Ingredients:

- 300g gluten-free all-purpose flour
- 5g baking powder
- 5g baking soda
- 3 ripe bananas, mashed
- 100g sugar
- 50g unsalted butter
- 2 eggs
- 100g chopped nuts

Directions

1. Preheat the oven to 350°F (175°C).
2. Grease a loaf pan.
3. In a bowl, combine gluten-free flour, baking powder, and baking soda.
4. In another bowl, cream together butter and sugar.
5. Beat in the eggs and mashed bananas.
6. Fold in the dry ingredients and chopped nuts.
7. Pour the batter into the prepared pan.
8. Bake for 60-65 minutes.
9. Enjoy the gluten-free twist on a classic.

Fun Fact

Banana bread is a beloved comfort food, and the addition of nuts provides a delightful crunch and flavor.

1 loaf

150 calories per serving

150 minutes

Quinoa and Chia Seed Bread (Gluten-Free)

Quinoa and Chia Seed Bread (Gluten-Free) is a hearty and nutritious bread made with quinoa and chia seeds. It's gluten-free and packed with protein and fiber.

Ingredients:

- 200g cooked quinoa
- 200g gluten-free all-purpose flour
- 50g chia seeds
- 5g baking powder
- 5g salt
- 250ml warm water
- 30ml olive oil

Directions

1. Preheat the oven to 350°F (175°C).
2. Grease a loaf pan.
3. In a bowl, mix cooked quinoa, gluten-free flour, chia seeds, baking powder, and salt.
4. In another bowl, whisk together warm water and olive oil.
5. Combine wet and dry ingredients.
6. Pour the batter into the prepared pan.
7. Bake for 45-50 minutes.
8. Enjoy the protein-packed goodness.

Fun Fact

Quinoa and chia seeds are rich in nutrients, making this bread a wholesome and nutritious option for a gluten-free diet.

12 biscuits

120 calories per serving

75 minutes

Sweet Potato Biscuits (Gluten-Free)

Ingredients:

- 200g sweet potato, mashed
- 200g gluten-free all-purpose flour
- 5g baking powder
- 5g salt
- 100ml milk
- 30ml olive oil
- 30g honey

Fun Fact

Sweet potato biscuits offer a unique twist on classic biscuits, with a touch of natural sweetness from the sweet potatoes.

Sweet Potato Biscuits (Gluten-Free) are soft and slightly sweet biscuits made with sweet potato. They are gluten-free and perfect as a side for soups and stews.

Directions

1. Preheat the oven to 425°F (220°C).
2. In a bowl, mix mashed sweet potato, gluten-free flour, baking powder, and salt.
3. In another bowl, combine milk, olive oil, and honey.
4. Combine wet and dry ingredients to form a dough.
5. Roll out the dough and cut out biscuits.
6. Place the biscuits on a baking sheet.
7. Bake for 15-18 minutes.
8. Enjoy the slightly sweet flavor of these biscuits.

4 flatbreads

110 calories per serving

60 minutes

Rice Flour Flatbread (Gluten-Free)

Ingredients:

- 200g rice flour
- 5g salt
- 150ml warm water
- 30ml olive oil

Fun Fact

Rice flour flatbreads are a common gluten-free alternative in many Asian cuisines and are used as a staple for various dishes

Rice Flour Flatbread (Gluten-Free) is a simple and versatile gluten-free bread made with rice flour. It's perfect for serving with a variety of dishes or as a wrap.

Directions

1. In a bowl, mix rice flour and salt.
2. Gradually add warm water and olive oil, stirring until the dough comes together.
3. Divide the dough into 4 portions.
4. Roll out each portion into a flatbread.
5. Heat a non-stick skillet over medium heat.
6. Cook the flatbreads, flipping until both sides are golden.
7. Serve as a side or as a wrap for your favorite fillings.

1 loaf

160 calories per serving

90 minutes

Zucchini Bread (Gluten-Free)

Zucchini Bread (Gluten-Free) is a moist and flavorful gluten-free bread that includes grated zucchini, adding both moisture and a hint of green goodness to each slice.

Ingredients:

- 300g gluten-free all-purpose flour
- 5g baking powder
- 5g baking soda
- 5g cinnamon
- 2 eggs
- 100g sugar
- 100ml olive oil
- 250g grated zucchini
- 50g chopped walnuts

Directions

1. Preheat the oven to 350°F (175°C).
2. Grease a loaf pan.
3. In a bowl, combine gluten-free flour, baking powder, baking soda, and cinnamon.
4. In another bowl, whisk together eggs, sugar, and olive oil.
5. Stir in grated zucchini and chopped walnuts.
6. Combine wet and dry ingredients.
7. Pour the batter into the prepared pan.
8. Bake for 50-55 minutes.
9. Enjoy the gluten-free zucchini goodness.

Fun Fact

Zucchini bread is a creative way to use up excess zucchini, and its subtle green color and moist texture make it a delightful treat.

Chapter 5: Quick and Easy No-Yeast Breads

1 loaf

120
calories
per
serving

60
minutes

Irish Brown Soda Bread

Ingredients:

- 200g whole wheat flour
- 200g all-purpose flour
- 5g baking soda
- 5g salt
- 350ml buttermilk

Irish Brown Soda Bread is a classic and hearty no-yeast bread from Ireland. It's dense and slightly sweet, perfect for serving with butter and a cup of tea.

Directions

1. Preheat the oven to 425°F (220°C).
2. In a bowl, combine whole wheat flour, all-purpose flour, baking soda, and salt.
3. Add buttermilk and mix to form a dough.
4. Shape the dough into a round loaf.
5. Place on a baking sheet and score a deep cross on top.
6. Bake for 15 minutes at 425°F, then reduce the oven to 400°F (200°C) and bake for an additional 15-20 minutes.
7. Enjoy the rustic flavors of Ireland.

Fun Fact

Irish Brown Soda Bread is a staple in Irish cuisine, often served as part of traditional meals.

1 loaf

140 calories per serving

50 minutes

Beer Bread

Ingredients:

- 300g all-purpose flour
- 5g salt
- 5g baking powder
- 50g sugar
- 330ml beer
- 30g melted butter

Beer Bread is a quick and easy no-yeast bread that's leavened with the help of beer. It has a slightly nutty flavor and pairs well with soups and stews.

Directions

1. Preheat the oven to 375°F (190°C).
2. Grease a loaf pan.
3. In a bowl, mix all-purpose flour, salt, baking powder, and sugar.
4. Stir in the beer to form a dough.
5. Pour the dough into the prepared pan.
6. Drizzle melted butter on top.
7. Bake for 45-50 minutes.
8. Enjoy the unique flavor of beer bread.

Fun Fact

Beer bread is a quick and versatile bread that can be made with different beer varieties, each imparting its own distinct flavor.

1 loaf

160 calories per serving

60 minutes

Cheddar and Chive Beer Bread

Cheddar and Chive Beer Bread is a cheesy and savory twist on traditional beer bread. It's loaded with cheddar cheese and fresh chives, making it a delightful appetizer.

Ingredients:

- 300g all-purpose flour
- 5g salt
- 5g baking powder
- 50g sugar
- 330ml beer
- 30g melted butter
- 100g cheddar cheese, shredded
- 2 tbsp fresh chives, chopped

Directions

1. Preheat the oven to 375°F (190°C).
2. Grease a loaf pan.
3. In a bowl, mix all-purpose flour, salt, baking powder, and sugar.
4. Stir in the beer to form a dough.
5. Fold in the shredded cheddar and chopped chives.
6. Pour the dough into the prepared pan.
7. Drizzle melted butter on top.
8. Bake for 45-50 minutes.
9. Enjoy the cheesy and savory goodness.

Fun Fact

Cheddar and Chive Beer Bread is a crowd-pleasing appetizer, perfect for parties and gatherings.

1 loaf

130 calories per serving

70 minutes

Irish Buttermilk Bread

Ingredients:

- 250g all-purpose flour
- 5g baking soda
- 5g salt
- 250ml buttermilk

Irish Buttermilk Bread is a traditional no-yeast bread from Ireland. It's simple and rustic, with a delightful buttermilk flavor and a golden crust.

Directions

1. Preheat the oven to 425°F (220°C).
2. In a bowl, mix all-purpose flour, baking soda, and salt.
3. Add buttermilk and mix to form a dough.
4. Shape the dough into a round loaf.
5. Place on a baking sheet and score a deep cross on top.
6. Bake for 15 minutes at 425°F, then reduce the oven to 400°F (200°C) and bake for an additional 25-30 minutes.
7. Enjoy the rustic flavors of Ireland.

Fun Fact

Irish Buttermilk Bread is a simple and traditional bread, often enjoyed with a spread of butter or jam.

1 loaf

170 calories per serving

60 minutes

No-Yeast Cheesy Herb Bread

No-Yeast Cheesy Herb Bread is a flavorful and aromatic bread that's loaded with herbs and cheese. It's perfect for dipping in soups or as a side for pasta dishes.

Ingredients:

- 300g all-purpose flour
- 5g baking powder
- 5g salt
- 50g grated parmesan cheese
- 1 tbsp dried herbs (e.g., basil, oregano, thyme)
- 250ml milk
- 30ml olive oil

Directions

1. Preheat the oven to 375°F (190°C).
2. Grease a loaf pan.
3. In a bowl, mix all-purpose flour, baking powder, salt, grated parmesan, and dried herbs.
4. Stir in milk and olive oil to form a dough.
5. Pour the dough into the prepared pan.
6. Bake for 45-50 minutes.
7. Enjoy the savory and cheesy flavors.

Fun Fact

No-Yeast Cheesy Herb Bread is a quick and flavorful bread that's perfect for adding a burst of flavor to your meal.

1 loaf

140 calories per serving

90 minutes

Oatmeal and Honey Bread

Oatmeal and Honey Bread is a hearty and wholesome no-yeast bread. It's made with oats and sweetened with honey, offering a nutty and slightly sweet flavor.

Ingredients:

- 200g all-purpose flour
- 100g rolled oats
- 5g baking soda
- 5g salt
- 250ml buttermilk
- 60ml honey
- 30ml olive oil

Directions

1. Preheat the oven to 350°F (175°C).
2. Grease a loaf pan.
3. In a bowl, mix all-purpose flour, rolled oats, baking soda, and salt.
4. In another bowl, combine buttermilk, honey, and olive oil.
5. Combine wet and dry ingredients to form a dough.
6. Pour the dough into the prepared pan.
7. Bake for 60-65 minutes.
8. Enjoy the hearty goodness.

Fun Fact

Oatmeal and Honey Bread is a nutritious and satisfying bread, perfect for breakfast or as a sandwich base.

4
flatbreads

90
calories
per
serving

45
minutes

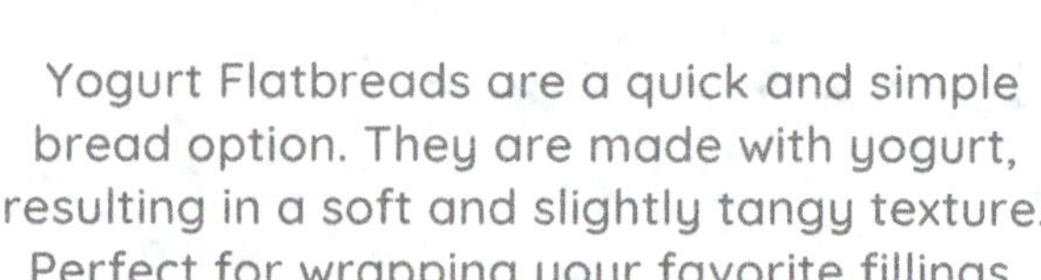

Yogurt Flatbreads

Ingredients:

- 200g all-purpose flour
- 5g salt
- 150g yogurt
- 30ml olive oil

Yogurt Flatbreads are a quick and simple bread option. They are made with yogurt, resulting in a soft and slightly tangy texture. Perfect for wrapping your favorite fillings.

Directions

1. In a bowl, mix all-purpose flour and salt.
2. Add yogurt and olive oil, stirring until the dough comes together.
3. Divide the dough into 4 portions.
4. Roll out each portion into a flatbread.
5. Heat a non-stick skillet over medium heat.
6. Cook the flatbreads, flipping until both sides are lightly browned.
7. Serve as a wrap for your favorite fillings.

Fun Fact

Yogurt flatbreads are a versatile and quick option for wraps and sandwiches. The yogurt adds a pleasant tanginess to the bread.

1 loaf

130 calories per serving

70 minutes

Irish Potato Bread

Irish Potato Bread is a traditional no-yeast bread from Ireland. It's made with mashed potatoes, resulting in a moist and slightly dense bread. Perfect with a pat of butter.

Ingredients:

- 200g all-purpose flour
- 5g baking soda
- 5g salt
- 250g mashed potatoes
- 250ml buttermilk

Directions

1. Preheat the oven to 425°F (220°C).
2. In a bowl, mix all-purpose flour, baking soda, and salt.
3. Add mashed potatoes and buttermilk to form a dough.
4. Shape the dough into a round loaf.
5. Place on a baking sheet and score a deep cross on top.
6. Bake for 15 minutes at 425°F, then reduce the oven to 400°F (200°C) and bake for an additional 25-30 minutes.
7. Enjoy the rustic flavors of Ireland.

Fun Fact

Irish Potato Bread is a comforting and traditional bread that's often served alongside soups and stews.

1 loaf

130 calories per serving

70 minutes

Whole Wheat Irish Soda Bread

Ingredients:

- 200g whole wheat flour
- 200g all-purpose flour
- 5g baking soda
- 5g salt
- 350ml buttermilk

Whole Wheat Irish Soda Bread is a healthier twist on the classic Irish soda bread. It's made with whole wheat flour, offering a nutty and wholesome flavor.

Directions

1. Preheat the oven to 425°F (220°C).
2. In a bowl, combine whole wheat flour, all-purpose flour, baking soda, and salt.
3. Add buttermilk and mix to form a dough.
4. Shape the dough into a round loaf.
5. Place on a baking sheet and score a deep cross on top.
6. Bake for 15 minutes at 425°F, then reduce the oven to 400°F (200°C) and bake for an additional 15-20 minutes.
7. Enjoy the nutty and whole wheat goodness.

Fun Fact

Whole Wheat Irish Soda Bread is a nutritious variation of the traditional Irish soda bread, offering a richer and nuttier flavor.

1 loaf

180 calories per serving

50 minutes

Rustic Beer and Cheese Bread

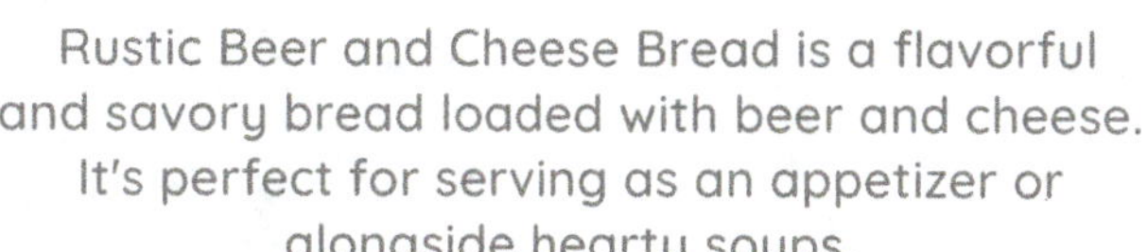

Rustic Beer and Cheese Bread is a flavorful and savory bread loaded with beer and cheese. It's perfect for serving as an appetizer or alongside hearty soups.

Ingredients:

- 300g all-purpose flour
- 5g baking powder
- 5g salt
- 330ml beer
- 30g melted butter
- 100g cheddar cheese, shredded
- 2 tbsp fresh herbs (e.g., rosemary, thyme)

Directions

1. Preheat the oven to 375°F (190°C).
2. Grease a loaf pan.
3. In a bowl, mix all-purpose flour, baking powder, salt, shredded cheddar, and fresh herbs.
4. Stir in the beer to form a dough.
5. Pour the dough into the prepared pan.
6. Drizzle melted butter on top.
7. Bake for 45-50 minutes.
8. Enjoy the savory and cheesy goodness.

Fun Fact

Rustic Beer and Cheese Bread is a crowd-pleasing appetizer, perfect for sharing and pairing with your favorite beverages.

We have a small favor to ask

As we delve into the heart of the "Breads Baking Made Easy: Knead to Know - Uncover the Secrets of Effortless Baking with Our 100+ Recipes Pictures Included," I want to take a moment to talk about something essential but often overlooked – reviews.

Reviews, my fellow bakers, are like the yeast in a perfectly risen loaf—crucial, often underestimated, and immensely rewarding. For a small publisher like us, they are the key ingredient that makes our creative efforts truly rise to the occasion.

If you find yourself enjoying the journey through these pages, I'd be grateful if you could take a moment to revisit the platform where you discovered this bread-baking adventure—whether it's an app or an online marketplace. There, much like the golden crust on a well-baked artisanal loaf, you'll encounter the review button. We would sincerely appreciate your honest rating and a brief, thoughtful sentence capturing your baking experience.

Every review is a pinch of salt for us, the element that enhances and brings out the flavors in our cookbook, and they mean more to us than the perfect crumb structure in a well-baked bread. In the spirit of transparency, should you stumble upon a minor hiccup within these pages, please know that we've mixed and kneaded our best efforts into this collection. We're not infallible, and, much like the occasional uneven rise, small mistakes can happen. We hope you can savor the overall baking experience despite these minor imperfections.

Your support, conveyed through a review, is like the perfect balance of ingredients in a successful bread recipe—it completes the experience and inspires us to keep crafting recipes that truly knead to your satisfaction. So, let your words be the extra dusting of flour on our baking masterpiece.

Now, as we return to the recipes, let the aroma of freshly baked bread fill your kitchen, and may each loaf be a testament to the joy and simplicity we've uncovered together. Happy baking!

Chapter 6: Breakfast Breads

1 loaf

190 calories per serving

90 minutes

Banana Nut Bread

Banana Nut Bread is a classic breakfast treat. It's moist, flavorful, and loaded with ripe bananas and chopped nuts. Perfect with a cup of coffee or tea.

Ingredients:

- 300g all-purpose flour
- 5g baking powder
- 5g baking soda
- 3 ripe bananas, mashed
- 100g sugar
- 50g unsalted butter
- 2 eggs
- 100g chopped nuts

Directions

1. Preheat the oven to 350°F (175°C).
2. Grease a loaf pan.
3. In a bowl, combine all-purpose flour, baking powder, and baking soda.
4. In another bowl, cream together butter and sugar.
5. Beat in the eggs and mashed bananas.
6. Fold in the dry ingredients and chopped nuts.
7. Pour the batter into the prepared pan.
8. Bake for 60-65 minutes.
9. Enjoy the classic goodness.

Fun Fact

Banana Nut Bread is a beloved breakfast bread with the delightful combination of bananas and nuts. It's a comforting and nostalgic treat.

1 loaf

160 calories per serving

90 minutes

Blueberry Lemon Zest Bread

Blueberry Lemon Zest Bread is a zesty and fruity breakfast bread. It's bursting with blueberries and has a refreshing lemon flavor. Perfect for a bright morning.

Ingredients:

- 300g all-purpose flour
- 5g baking powder
- 5g baking soda
- Zest of 1 lemon
- 200g blueberries
- 100g sugar
- 50g unsalted butter
- 2 eggs

Directions

1. Preheat the oven to 350°F (175°C).
2. Grease a loaf pan.
3. In a bowl, combine all-purpose flour, baking powder, and baking soda.
4. Add lemon zest and blueberries, tossing them in some flour.
5. In another bowl, cream together butter and sugar.
6. Beat in the eggs.
7. Fold in the dry ingredients and blueberries.
8. Pour the batter into the prepared pan.
9. Bake for 60-65 minutes.
10. Enjoy the zesty and fruity flavors.

Fun Fact

Blueberry Lemon Zest Bread offers a refreshing and tangy twist on traditional breakfast bread, making it a delightful morning treat.

1 loaf

170 calories per serving

90 minutes

Chocolate Chip Zucchini Bread

Ingredients:

- 300g all-purpose flour
- 5g baking powder
- 5g baking soda
- 200g grated zucchini
- 100g sugar
- 50g unsalted butter
- 2 eggs
- 100g chocolate chips

Fun Fact

Chocolate Chip Zucchini Bread is a clever and delicious way to incorporate vegetables into your breakfast. The chocolate chips add a sweet touch.

Chocolate Chip Zucchini Bread is a sneaky way to enjoy vegetables for breakfast. It's moist, sweet, and studded with chocolate chips. A family favorite.

Directions

1. Preheat the oven to 350°F (175°C).
2. Grease a loaf pan.
3. In a bowl, combine all-purpose flour, baking powder, and baking soda.
4. Squeeze excess moisture from grated zucchini.
5. In another bowl, cream together butter and sugar.
6. Beat in the eggs.
7. Fold in the dry ingredients, grated zucchini, and chocolate chips.
8. Pour the batter into the prepared pan.
9. Bake for 60-65 minutes.
10. Enjoy the hidden veggie goodness.

1 loaf

160 calories per serving

120 minutes

Cinnamon Swirl Bread

Ingredients:

- 300g all-purpose flour
- 5g baking powder
- 5g baking soda
- 100g sugar
- 50g unsalted butter
- 2 eggs
- 5g ground cinnamon

Fun Fact

Cinnamon Swirl Bread is a comforting and spiced breakfast bread, perfect for creating a warm and cozy atmosphere in the morning.

Cinnamon Swirl Bread is a warmly spiced breakfast bread. It's swirled with a sweet cinnamon filling, making each slice a cozy delight. Best enjoyed toasted with butter.

Directions

1. Preheat the oven to 350°F (175°C).
2. Grease a loaf pan.
3. In a bowl, combine all-purpose flour, baking powder, and baking soda.
4. In another bowl, cream together butter and sugar.
5. Beat in the eggs.
6. In a small bowl, mix ground cinnamon and a bit of sugar to create the filling.
7. Pour half of the batter into the prepared pan.
8. Sprinkle the cinnamon filling.
9. Top with the remaining batter.
10. Use a knife to create swirls.
11. Bake for 60-65 minutes.
12. Enjoy the cozy cinnamon goodness.

1 loaf

150 calories per serving

90 minutes

Cranberry Orange Bread

Cranberry Orange Bread is a fruity and tangy breakfast bread. It's packed with dried cranberries and has a zesty orange flavor. Ideal for a bright and flavorful start.

Ingredients:

- 300g all-purpose flour
- 5g baking powder
- 5g baking soda
- Zest of 1 orange
- 200g dried cranberries
- 100g sugar
- 50g unsalted butter
- 2 eggs

Directions

1. Preheat the oven to 350°F (175°C).
2. Grease a loaf pan.
3. In a bowl, combine all-purpose flour, baking powder, and baking soda.
4. Add orange zest and dried cranberries, tossing them in some flour.
5. In another bowl, cream together butter and sugar.
6. Beat in the eggs.
7. Fold in the dry ingredients and cranberries.
8. Pour the batter into the prepared pan.
9. Bake for 60-65 minutes.
10. Enjoy the fruity and tangy flavors.

Fun Fact

Cranberry Orange Bread is a vibrant and flavorful breakfast bread, combining the sweet-tartness of cranberries and the zest of orange.

1 loaf

200 calories per serving

90 minutes

Nutella Swirl Banana Bread

Nutella Swirl Banana Bread is a decadent twist on traditional banana bread. It's generously swirled with creamy Nutella, making it an indulgent breakfast treat.

Ingredients:

- 300g all-purpose flour
- 5g baking powder
- 5g baking soda
- 3 ripe bananas, mashed
- 100g sugar
- 50g unsalted butter
- 2 eggs
- 100g Nutella

Directions

1. Preheat the oven to 350°F (175°C).
2. Grease a loaf pan.
3. In a bowl, combine all-purpose flour, baking powder, and baking soda.
4. In another bowl, cream together butter and sugar.
5. Beat in the eggs and mashed bananas.
6. Pour half of the banana bread batter into the prepared pan.
7. Add spoonfuls of Nutella and swirl it into the batter.
8. Top with the remaining batter.
9. Bake for 60-65 minutes.
10. Enjoy the delightful Nutella twist.

Fun Fact

Nutella Swirl Banana Bread is a delightful combination of bananas and the beloved hazelnut-chocolate spread, Nutella. It's perfect for those with a sweet tooth.

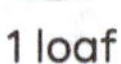

1 loaf

180 calories per serving

90 minutes

Pumpkin Chocolate Chip Bread

Ingredients:

- 300g all-purpose flour
- 5g baking powder
- 5g baking soda
- 200g pumpkin puree
- 100g sugar
- 50g unsalted butter
- 2 eggs
- 100g chocolate chips

Pumpkin Chocolate Chip Bread is a fall-inspired breakfast bread. It's infused with pumpkin puree and studded with chocolate chips, creating a comforting and sweet treat.

Directions

1. Preheat the oven to 350°F (175°C).
2. Grease a loaf pan.
3. In a bowl, combine all-purpose flour, baking powder, and baking soda.
4. In another bowl, cream together butter and sugar.
5. Beat in the eggs and pumpkin puree.
6. Fold in the dry ingredients and chocolate chips.
7. Pour the batter into the prepared pan.
8. Bake for 60-65 minutes.
9. Enjoy the warm and chocolaty flavors.

Fun Fact

Pumpkin Chocolate Chip Bread is a cozy and seasonal breakfast bread that's perfect for autumn mornings. The chocolate chips add a delightful touch.

1 loaf

170 calories per serving

90 minutes

Cherry Almond Bread

Ingredients:

- 300g all-purpose flour
- 5g baking powder
- 5g baking soda
- 200g dried cherries
- 50g ground almonds
- 100g sugar
- 50g unsalted butter
- 2 eggs

Fun Fact

Cherry Almond Bread is a lovely and elegant breakfast bread, combining the sweetness of cherries with the subtle nuttiness of almonds.

Cherry Almond Bread is a delightful and fruity breakfast bread. It's packed with dried cherries and has a subtle almond flavor, creating a lovely and nutty combination.

Directions

1. Preheat the oven to 350°F (175°C).
2. Grease a loaf pan.
3. In a bowl, combine all-purpose flour, baking powder, and baking soda.
4. In another bowl, cream together butter and sugar.
5. Beat in the eggs.
6. Fold in the dry ingredients, dried cherries, and ground almonds.
7. Pour the batter into the prepared pan.
8. Bake for 60-65 minutes.
9. Enjoy the fruity and nutty goodness.

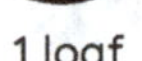

1 loaf

190
calories
per
serving

90
minutes

Walnut and Fig Bread

Walnut and Fig Bread is a sophisticated and flavorful breakfast bread. It's enriched with chopped walnuts and dried figs, creating a delightful combination of textures and flavors.

Ingredients:

- 300g all-purpose flour
- 5g baking powder
- 5g baking soda
- 100g dried figs, chopped
- 100g chopped walnuts
- 100g sugar
- 50g unsalted butter
- 2 eggs

Directions

1. Preheat the oven to 350°F (175°C).
2. Grease a loaf pan.
3. In a bowl, combine all-purpose flour, baking powder, and baking soda.
4. In another bowl, cream together butter and sugar.
5. Beat in the eggs.
6. Fold in the dry ingredients, dried figs, and chopped walnuts.
7. Pour the batter into the prepared pan.
8. Bake for 60-65 minutes.
9. Enjoy the sophisticated nutty and fruity blend.

Fun Fact

Walnut and Fig Bread is a delightful and upscale breakfast bread, perfect for those who appreciate the combination of nuts and dried fruits.

1 loaf

200 calories per serving

90 minutes

Apple Cider Donut Bread

Apple Cider Donut Bread is a fall-inspired delight. It's infused with apple cider and warm spices, reminiscent of a classic apple cider donut. Perfect for a cozy morning.

Ingredients:

- 300g all-purpose flour
- 5g baking powder
- 5g baking soda
- 240ml apple cider
- 100g sugar
- 50g unsalted butter
- 2 eggs
- 5g ground cinnamon
- 2g ground nutmeg

Directions

1. Preheat the oven to 350°F (175°C).
2. Grease a loaf pan.
3. In a bowl, combine all-purpose flour, baking powder, and baking soda.
4. In another bowl, cream together butter and sugar.
5. Beat in the eggs.
6. Stir in apple cider, ground cinnamon, and ground nutmeg.
7. Fold in the dry ingredients.
8. Pour the batter into the prepared pan.
9. Bake for 60-65 minutes.
10. Enjoy the cozy and spiced flavors.

Fun Fact

Apple Cider Donut Bread captures the essence of autumn with the flavors of apple cider and warm spices. It's a perfect treat for fall mornings.

Chapter 7: Holiday Specials

1 loaf

220 calories per serving

150 minutes

Stollen - German Christmas Bread

Ingredients:

- 400g all-purpose flour
- 10g active dry yeast
- 100g sugar
- 200g butter, softened
- 200g mixed dried fruits (raisins, currants, candied peel)
- 100g chopped nuts (almonds, hazelnuts)
- 100g marzipan
- 240ml milk
- Zest of 1 lemon
- 5g ground cinnamon
- 5g ground nutmeg
- A pinch of salt
- Powdered sugar (for dusting)

Fun Fact

Stollen is a cherished German Christmas tradition, symbolizing the baby Jesus wrapped in swaddling clothes. It's a sweet and festive bread enjoyed during the holiday season.

Stollen is a beloved German Christmas bread, traditionally enjoyed during the holiday season. It's enriched with dried fruits, nuts, and marzipan, creating a delightful and festive treat.

Directions

1. In a bowl, dissolve yeast in warm milk and let it proof.
2. In a large bowl, mix flour, sugar, salt, lemon zest, ground cinnamon, and ground nutmeg.
3. Cut in the softened butter.
4. Stir in proofed yeast mixture.
5. Knead the dough until smooth, then add dried fruits and chopped nuts.
6. Let the dough rise until doubled in size.
7. Roll out the dough and place a log of marzipan in the center.
8. Fold the dough over the marzipan, sealing it.
9. Shape it into a loaf.
10. Let it rise again.
11. Bake until golden brown.
12. Dust with powdered sugar.
13. Enjoy this German Christmas tradition.

1 loaf

230 calories per serving

180 minutes

Panettone - Italian Christmas Bread

Ingredients:

- 500g all-purpose flour
- 10g active dry yeast
- 200g sugar
- 150g butter, softened
- 200g mixed dried fruits (raisins, candied orange peel)
- 3 eggs
- 120ml milk
- Zest of 1 lemon
- Zest of 1 orange
- 5g salt
- Powdered sugar (for dusting)

Fun Fact

Panettone is a traditional Italian Christmas bread, beloved for its fruity and aromatic crumb. It's a festive staple during the holiday season in Italy and beyond.

Panettone is a classic Italian Christmas bread, known for its tall, domed shape and fruity, fragrant crumb. It's a staple during the holiday season in Italy.

Directions

1. In a bowl, dissolve yeast in warm milk and let it proof.
2. In a large bowl, mix flour, sugar, salt, lemon zest, and orange zest.
3. Cut in the softened butter.
4. Stir in proofed yeast mixture.
5. Knead the dough until smooth, then add dried fruits.
6. Let the dough rise until doubled in size.
7. Beat eggs and add them to the dough.
8. Let the dough rise again.
9. Bake until golden brown.
10. Dust with powdered sugar.
11. Enjoy this Italian Christmas tradition.

12 buns

160 calories per bun

120 minutes

Hot Cross Buns

Ingredients:

- 500g all-purpose flour
- 10g active dry yeast
- 50g sugar
- 50g butter, melted
- 200ml milk
- 1 egg
- 100g mixed dried fruits (raisins, currants)
- 5g ground cinnamon
- 2g ground nutmeg
- A pinch of salt
- Icing sugar (for the cross)

Fun Fact

Hot Cross Buns are a symbol of Good Friday, known for their spiced and sweet nature. They are a delightful Easter tradition.

Hot Cross Buns are spiced and sweet buns traditionally enjoyed on Good Friday. They are marked with a cross on top and have a delightful mix of raisins and currants.

Directions

1. In a bowl, dissolve yeast in warm milk and let it proof.
2. In a large bowl, mix flour, sugar, salt, ground cinnamon, and ground nutmeg.
3. Cut in the melted butter.
4. Stir in proofed yeast mixture and the egg.
5. Knead the dough until smooth, then add dried fruits.
6. Let the dough rise until doubled in size.
7. Divide the dough into 12 portions and shape them into buns.
8. Place buns on a baking sheet and let them rise again.
9. Preheat the oven and bake until golden brown.
10. After baking, create the cross with icing sugar.
11. Enjoy these traditional buns.

 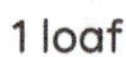  

1 loaf

200 calories per serving

150 minutes

Easter Braided Bread

Ingredients:

- 500g all-purpose flour
- 10g active dry yeast
- 50g sugar
- 50g butter, melted
- 200ml milk
- 3 eggs
- A pinch of salt
- Colored sprinkles (for decoration)

Easter Braided Bread is a beautiful and symbolic bread often baked for Easter Sunday. Its braided design and sweet taste make it a festive centerpiece.

Directions

1. In a bowl, dissolve yeast in warm milk and let it proof.
2. In a large bowl, mix flour, sugar, and salt.
3. Cut in the melted butter.
4. Stir in proofed yeast mixture and the eggs.
5. Knead the dough until smooth.
6. Let the dough rise until doubled in size.
7. Divide the dough into 3 portions and braid them together.
8. Place the braided loaf on a baking sheet.
9. Let it rise again.
10. Preheat the oven and bake until golden brown.
11. Decorate with colored sprinkles.
12. Enjoy this festive Easter bread.

Fun Fact

Easter Braided Bread is a visually stunning and festive bread, often baked to celebrate Easter. It's a symbol of joy and renewal.

12 rolls

140 calories per roll

120 minutes

Thanksgiving Pumpkin Rolls

Ingredients:

- 500g all-purpose flour
- 10g active dry yeast
- 50g sugar
- 50g butter, melted
- 200ml milk
- 150g pumpkin puree
- 5g ground cinnamon
- 2g ground nutmeg
- A pinch of salt

Fun Fact

Thanksgiving Pumpkin Rolls are a wonderful addition to your holiday table, infused with the flavors of pumpkin and spices, making them perfect for Thanksgiving.

Thanksgiving Pumpkin Rolls are soft and flavorful dinner rolls with a hint of pumpkin and warm spices. They are a delightful addition to your Thanksgiving table.

Directions

1. In a bowl, dissolve yeast in warm milk and let it proof.
2. In a large bowl, mix flour, sugar, salt, ground cinnamon, and ground nutmeg.
3. Cut in the melted butter.
4. Stir in proofed yeast mixture and the pumpkin puree.
5. Knead the dough until smooth.
6. Let the dough rise until doubled in size.
7. Divide the dough into 12 portions and shape them into rolls.
8. Place rolls on a baking sheet and let them rise again.
9. Preheat the oven and bake until golden brown.
10. Enjoy these Thanksgiving dinner rolls.

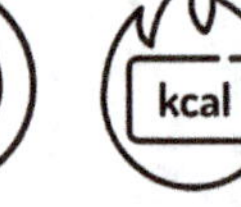

1 loaf

180 calories per serving

120 minutes

Valentine's Day Heart-Shaped Bread

Valentine's Day Heart-Shaped Bread is a lovely and romantic way to celebrate the day of love. This bread is shaped like a heart and can be a heartfelt gift for your loved one.

Ingredients:

- 400g all-purpose flour
- 10g active dry yeast
- 50g sugar
- 50g butter, softened
- 200ml milk
- 1 egg
- A pinch of salt
- Red food coloring (optional)

Directions

1. In a bowl, dissolve yeast in warm milk and let it proof.
2. In a large bowl, mix flour, sugar, and salt.
3. Cut in the softened butter.
4. Stir in proofed yeast mixture and the egg.
5. Knead the dough until smooth.
6. Add red food coloring if desired.
7. Let the dough rise until doubled in size.
8. Shape the dough into a heart.
9. Let it rise again.
10. Preheat the oven and bake until golden brown.
11. Share this heartwarming bread with your Valentine.

Fun Fact

Valentine's Day Heart-Shaped Bread is a delightful way to express your love and appreciation on Valentine's Day. It's a heartfelt gesture in the form of a delicious bread.

1 loaf

170 calories per serving

150 minutes

Halloween Spiderweb Bread

Halloween Spiderweb Bread is a spooky and fun bread to serve during Halloween celebrations. It's adorned with a spiderweb design made of black dough, creating a creepy yet tasty treat.

Ingredients:

- 400g all-purpose flour
- 10g active dry yeast
- 50g sugar
- 50g butter, melted
- 200ml milk
- Black food coloring
- A pinch of salt

Directions

1. In a bowl, dissolve yeast in warm milk and let it proof.
2. In a large bowl, mix flour, sugar, and salt.
3. Cut in the melted butter.
4. Stir in proofed yeast mixture.
5. Knead the dough until smooth.
6. Add black food coloring to a portion of the dough.
7. Shape the black dough into a spiderweb design on top of the bread.
8. Let the dough rise until doubled in size.
9. Preheat the oven and bake until golden brown.
10. Serve this spooky treat on Halloween.

Fun Fact

Halloween Spiderweb Bread is a spooky and creative addition to your Halloween spread, making it a fun and eerie centerpiece for the occasion.

1 loaf

190 calories per serving

150 minutes

Rosh Hashanah Honey Challah

Ingredients:

- 500g all-purpose flour
- 10g active dry yeast
- 100g sugar
- 50g butter, melted
- 2 eggs
- 120ml warm water
- 120ml honey
- A pinch of salt
- Sesame seeds (for topping)

Fun Fact

Rosh Hashanah Honey Challah is a meaningful and sweet bread, symbolizing the hope for a sweet and prosperous year. It's a significant part of Rosh Hashanah celebrations.

Rosh Hashanah Honey Challah is a sweet and symbolic bread traditionally enjoyed during the Jewish New Year. It's enriched with honey, symbolizing a sweet year ahead.

Directions

1. In a bowl, dissolve yeast in warm water and let it proof with a bit of sugar.
2. In a large bowl, mix flour, remaining sugar, and salt.
3. Cut in the melted butter.
4. Stir in proofed yeast mixture and the eggs.
5. Knead the dough until smooth.
6. Let the dough rise until doubled in size.
7. Braid the dough into a traditional challah shape.
8. Let it rise again.
9. Preheat the oven and brush the bread with honey.
10. Sprinkle sesame seeds on top.
11. Bake until golden brown.
12. Enjoy this sweet and symbolic bread.

1 loaf

220 calories per serving

150 minutes

Diwali Sweet Bread

Diwali Sweet Bread is a celebratory and sweet bread often enjoyed during the festival of lights. It's flavored with aromatic spices and enriched with dried fruits and nuts.

Ingredients:

- 500g all-purpose flour
- 10g active dry yeast
- 100g sugar
- 50g ghee (clarified butter)
- 200ml warm milk
- 1 tsp cardamom powder
- 50g mixed dried fruits and nuts
- A pinch of salt

Directions

1. In a bowl, dissolve yeast in warm milk and let it proof with a bit of sugar.
2. In a large bowl, mix flour, remaining sugar, cardamom powder, and salt.
3. Cut in the ghee.
4. Stir in proofed yeast mixture.
5. Knead the dough until smooth, then add dried fruits and nuts.
6. Let the dough rise until doubled in size.
7. Shape the dough into a loaf.
8. Let it rise again.
9. Preheat the oven and bake until golden brown.
10. Enjoy this sweet and fragrant bread during Diwali celebrations.

Fun Fact

Diwali Sweet Bread is a fragrant and delightful addition to your Diwali festivities. It's a symbol of sweetness and abundance during the festival of lights.

12
sufganiyot

190
calories per sufganiyah

120
minutes

Hanukkah Sufganiyot

Ingredients:

- 500g all-purpose flour
- 10g active dry yeast
- 100g sugar
- 50g butter, melted
- 2 eggs
- 200ml warm milk
- Fruit jam (your choice of flavor)
- Powdered sugar (for dusting)

Fun Fact

Hanukkah Sufganiyot are a beloved Hanukkah tradition, symbolizing the miracle of the oil. They are filled with fruity goodness and a delightful way to celebrate the Festival of Lights.

Hanukkah Sufganiyot are sweet and jelly-filled doughnuts traditionally enjoyed during Hanukkah, the Festival of Lights. They are a delicious and indulgent treat.

Directions

1. In a bowl, dissolve yeast in warm milk and let it proof with a bit of sugar.
2. In a large bowl, mix flour, remaining sugar, and salt.
3. Cut in the melted butter.
4. Stir in proofed yeast mixture and the eggs.
5. Knead the dough until smooth.
6. Let the dough rise until doubled in size.
7. Roll out the dough and cut rounds.
8. Let the rounds rise again.
9. Heat oil for frying.
10. Fry until golden brown, then fill with fruit jam.
11. Dust with powdered sugar.
12. Enjoy these delectable Hanukkah treats.

Chapter 8: Healthy and Whole Grain Breads

1 loaf

160 calories per serving

120 minutes

Quinoa and Chia Seed Bread

Ingredients:

- 400g whole wheat flour
- 10g active dry yeast
- 50g quinoa
- 20g chia seeds
- 5g honey
- 5g salt
- 300ml warm water

Quinoa and Chia Seed Bread is a nutritious and protein-packed bread, enriched with the goodness of quinoa and chia seeds. It's a wholesome choice for health-conscious individuals.

Directions

1. In a bowl, dissolve yeast in warm water and let it proof with a bit of honey.
2. In a large bowl, mix whole wheat flour, quinoa, chia seeds, and salt.
3. Stir in proofed yeast mixture.
4. Knead the dough until smooth.
5. Let the dough rise until doubled in size.
6. Shape the dough into a loaf.
7. Let it rise again.
8. Preheat the oven and bake until golden brown.
9. Enjoy this nutritious and seedy bread.

Fun Fact

Quinoa and Chia Seed Bread is a wholesome and protein-rich choice for those seeking a nutritious bread option. It's a delicious way to incorporate superfoods into your diet.

1 loaf

150 calories per serving

120 minutes

Whole Wheat Sunflower Seed Bread

Ingredients:

- 400g whole wheat flour
- 10g active dry yeast
- 50g sunflower seeds
- 5g honey
- 5g salt
- 300ml warm water

Whole Wheat Sunflower Seed Bread is a hearty and fiber-rich bread, brimming with the nutty goodness of sunflower seeds. It's a great choice for those looking for a wholesome bread.

Directions

1. In a bowl, dissolve yeast in warm water and let it proof with a bit of honey.
2. In a large bowl, mix whole wheat flour, sunflower seeds, and salt.
3. Stir in proofed yeast mixture.
4. Knead the dough until smooth.
5. Let the dough rise until doubled in size.
6. Shape the dough into a loaf.
7. Let it rise again.
8. Preheat the oven and bake until golden brown.
9. Enjoy this fiber-packed bread with a nutty crunch.

Fun Fact

Whole Wheat Sunflower Seed Bread is a nutritious and hearty choice, perfect for those who appreciate the wholesome goodness of sunflower seeds in their bread.

1 loaf

170 calories per serving

150 minutes

Multigrain Bread

Multigrain Bread is a versatile and nutrient-rich bread, featuring a medley of grains and seeds. It's a balanced choice for those looking to incorporate a variety of grains into their diet.

Ingredients:

- 400g whole wheat flour
- 10g active dry yeast
- 50g mixed grains and seeds (oats, flaxseeds, sesame seeds, etc.)
- 5g honey
- 5g salt
- 300ml warm water

Directions

1. In a bowl, dissolve yeast in warm water and let it proof with a bit of honey.
2. In a large bowl, mix whole wheat flour, mixed grains and seeds, and salt.
3. Stir in proofed yeast mixture.
4. Knead the dough until smooth.
5. Let the dough rise until doubled in size.
6. Shape the dough into a loaf.
7. Let it rise again.
8. Preheat the oven and bake until golden brown.
9. Enjoy this medley of grains and seeds.

Fun Fact

Multigrain Bread is a well-balanced and nutritious choice, providing a variety of grains and seeds in one delicious loaf. It's a great addition to a healthy diet.

1 loaf

160 calories per serving

120 minutes

Oat and Honey Bread

Oat and Honey Bread is a simple and wholesome bread, combining the nutty flavor of oats with the sweetness of honey. It's a delightful and comforting choice for all ages.

Ingredients:

- 400g whole wheat flour
- 10g active dry yeast
- 50g rolled oats
- 10g honey
- 5g salt
- 300ml warm water

Directions

1. In a bowl, dissolve yeast in warm water and let it proof with a bit of honey.
2. In a large bowl, mix whole wheat flour, rolled oats, and salt.
3. Stir in proofed yeast mixture.
4. Knead the dough until smooth.
5. Let the dough rise until doubled in size.
6. Shape the dough into a loaf.
7. Let it rise again.
8. Preheat the oven and bake until golden brown.
9. Enjoy this comforting and hearty bread.

Fun Fact

Oat and Honey Bread is a simple and heartwarming choice, perfect for those who appreciate the comforting flavors of oats and honey in their bread.

1 loaf

180 calories per serving

150 minutes

Flaxseed and Walnut Bread

Ingredients:

- 400g whole wheat flour
- 10g active dry yeast
- 50g flaxseeds
- 50g chopped walnuts
- 5g honey
- 5g salt
- 300ml warm water

Flaxseed and Walnut Bread is a nutritious and omega-3-rich bread, loaded with the goodness of flaxseeds and walnuts. It's a great choice for those seeking a brain-boosting bread.

Directions

1. In a bowl, dissolve yeast in warm water and let it proof with a bit of honey.
2. In a large bowl, mix whole wheat flour, flaxseeds, chopped walnuts, and salt.
3. Stir in proofed yeast mixture.
4. Knead the dough until smooth.
5. Let the dough rise until doubled in size.
6. Shape the dough into a loaf.
7. Let it rise again.
8. Preheat the oven and bake until golden brown.
9. Enjoy this brain-boosting and nutty bread.

Fun Fact

Flaxseed and Walnut Bread is a nutritious and omega-3-rich choice, perfect for those who prioritize brain-boosting ingredients in their daily bread.

1 loaf

140 calories per serving

150 minutes

100% Whole Wheat Bread

Ingredients:

- 500g whole wheat flour
- 10g active dry yeast
- 5g sugar
- 5g salt
- 350ml warm water

100% Whole Wheat Bread is a hearty and fiber-rich bread, made entirely from whole wheat flour. It's a nutritious choice for those who value the goodness of whole grains.

Directions

1. In a bowl, dissolve yeast in warm water and let it proof with a bit of sugar.
2. In a large bowl, mix whole wheat flour and salt.
3. Stir in proofed yeast mixture.
4. Knead the dough until smooth.
5. Let the dough rise until doubled in size.
6. Shape the dough into a loaf.
7. Let it rise again.
8. Preheat the oven and bake until golden brown.
9. Enjoy this 100% whole wheat goodness.

Fun Fact

100% Whole Wheat Bread is a nutritious and straightforward choice for those who appreciate the purity of whole wheat in their bread. It's a wholesome staple.

1 loaf

160 calories per serving

120 minutes

Spelt and Honey Bread

Ingredients:

- 400g spelt flour
- 10g active dry yeast
- 50g honey
- 5g salt
- 250ml warm water

Spelt and Honey Bread is a delightful and slightly nutty bread, combining the earthy flavor of spelt with the sweetness of honey. It's a flavorful and wholesome choice.

Directions

1. In a bowl, dissolve yeast in warm water and let it proof with honey.
2. In a large bowl, mix spelt flour and salt.
3. Stir in proofed yeast mixture.
4. Knead the dough until smooth.
5. Let the dough rise until doubled in size.
6. Shape the dough into a loaf.
7. Let it rise again.
8. Preheat the oven and bake until golden brown.
9. Enjoy this nutty and sweet bread.

Fun Fact

Spelt and Honey Bread is a flavorful and nutty choice for those who appreciate the unique taste of spelt and the sweetness of honey in their bread.

1 loaf

150 calories per serving

180 minutes

Sprouted Grain Bread

Ingredients:

- 400g sprouted grain flour
- 10g active dry yeast
- 5g sugar
- 5g salt
- 300ml warm water

Fun Fact

Sprouted Grain Bread is a power-packed and nutritious choice, perfect for those who seek the benefits of sprouted grains and seeds in their daily bread.

Sprouted Grain Bread is a wholesome and nutrient-rich bread, made from sprouted grains and seeds. It's a power-packed choice for those who prioritize nutrition.

Directions

1. In a bowl, dissolve yeast in warm water and let it proof with sugar.
2. In a large bowl, mix sprouted grain flour and salt.
3. Stir in proofed yeast mixture.
4. Knead the dough until smooth.
5. Let the dough rise until doubled in size.
6. Shape the dough into a loaf.
7. Let it rise again.
8. Preheat the oven and bake until golden brown.
9. Enjoy this nutrient-rich bread.

1 loaf

170 calories per serving

150 minutes

Amaranth and Millet Bread

Amaranth and Millet Bread is a unique and protein-rich bread, combining the goodness of amaranth and millet. It's a wholesome choice for those looking for alternative grains.

Ingredients:

- 400g amaranth flour
- 10g active dry yeast
- 50g millet
- 5g salt
- 300ml warm water

Directions

1. In a bowl, dissolve yeast in warm water.
2. In a large bowl, mix amaranth flour, millet, and salt.
3. Stir in proofed yeast mixture.
4. Knead the dough until smooth.
5. Let the dough rise until doubled in size.
6. Shape the dough into a loaf.
7. Let it rise again.
8. Preheat the oven and bake until golden brown.
9. Enjoy this alternative grain bread.

Fun Fact

Amaranth and Millet Bread is a unique and protein-rich choice, perfect for those who appreciate the flavors and nutrition of amaranth and millet in their bread.

1 loaf

180 calories per serving

150 minutes

Kamut and Date Bread

Kamut and Date Bread is a flavorful and nutrient-packed bread, combining the ancient grain Kamut with the sweetness of dates. It's a delightful and nutritious choice.

Ingredients:

- 400g Kamut flour
- 10g active dry yeast
- 100g chopped dates
- 5g salt
- 300ml warm water

Directions

1. In a bowl, dissolve yeast in warm water.
2. In a large bowl, mix Kamut flour, chopped dates, and salt.
3. Stir in proofed yeast mixture.
4. Knead the dough until smooth.
5. Let the dough rise until doubled in size.
6. Shape the dough into a loaf.
7. Let it rise again.
8. Preheat the oven and bake until golden brown.
9. Enjoy this flavorful and ancient grain bread.

Fun Fact

Kamut and Date Bread is a delightful and nutrient-packed choice, perfect for those who appreciate the unique taste of Kamut and the natural sweetness of dates in their bread.

Chapter 9: Quick Breads and Muffins

12
muffins

180
calories
per
muffin

45
minutes

Banana Nut Muffins

Banana Nut Muffins are moist and flavorful, made with ripe bananas and crunchy walnuts. They are a delightful way to start your day with a touch of sweetness.

Ingredients:

- 2 ripe bananas, mashed
- 150g sugar
- 1 egg
- 60ml vegetable oil
- 5g baking powder
- 5g baking soda
- 2g salt
- 200g all-purpose flour
- 100g chopped walnuts

Directions

1. Preheat the oven and line a muffin tin with paper liners.
2. In a bowl, mix mashed bananas, sugar, egg, and vegetable oil.
3. In another bowl, whisk together baking powder, baking soda, salt, and flour.
4. Combine wet and dry ingredients, then fold in chopped walnuts.
5. Fill each muffin cup 2/3 full.
6. Bake until a toothpick comes out clean.
7. Enjoy these moist and nutty muffins.

Fun Fact

Banana Nut Muffins are a classic and comforting breakfast treat, perfect for those who love the combination of ripe bananas and crunchy walnuts in a muffin.

12
muffins

150
calories
per
muffin

40
minutes

Lemon Blueberry Muffins

Lemon Blueberry Muffins are light and tangy, filled with juicy blueberries and zesty lemon flavor. They are a refreshing and delightful morning indulgence.

Ingredients:

- 200g all-purpose flour
- 150g sugar
- 1 egg
- 80ml vegetable oil
- 120ml milk
- 5g baking powder
- 2g salt
- 150g blueberries
- Zest of 1 lemon
- Juice of 1 lemon

Directions

1. Preheat the oven and line a muffin tin with paper liners.
2. In a bowl, mix sugar, egg, vegetable oil, and milk.
3. In another bowl, whisk together flour, baking powder, salt, and lemon zest.
4. Combine wet and dry ingredients, then fold in blueberries and lemon juice.
5. Fill each muffin cup 2/3 full.
6. Bake until golden brown.
7. Enjoy these zesty and fruity muffins.

Fun Fact

Lemon Blueberry Muffins are a refreshing and tangy morning treat, perfect for those who enjoy the combination of blueberries and lemon in a muffin.

1 loaf | 200 calories per serving | 60 minutes

Chocolate Zucchini Bread

Chocolate Zucchini Bread is a moist and chocolaty delight that sneaks in the goodness of zucchini. It's a sweet and chocolatey treat for any time of day.

Ingredients:

- 200g all-purpose flour
- 50g cocoa powder
- 150g sugar
- 2 eggs
- 120ml vegetable oil
- 5g baking powder
- 5g baking soda
- 2g salt
- 200g grated zucchini
- 100g chocolate chips

Directions

1. Preheat the oven and grease a loaf pan.
2. In a bowl, mix sugar, eggs, and vegetable oil.
3. In another bowl, whisk together flour, cocoa powder, baking powder, baking soda, and salt.
4. Combine wet and dry ingredients, then fold in grated zucchini and chocolate chips.
5. Transfer the batter to the loaf pan.
6. Bake until a toothpick comes out clean.
7. Enjoy this moist and chocolatey bread.

Fun Fact

Chocolate Zucchini Bread is a clever and chocolaty treat, perfect for those who want to enjoy the rich taste of chocolate while sneaking in some zucchini goodness.

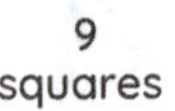

9
squares

150
calories
per
serving

30
minutes

Cornbread

Ingredients:

- 150g cornmeal
- 150g all-purpose flour
- 50g sugar
- 5g baking powder
- 2g salt
- 1 egg
- 250ml milk
- 60ml vegetable oil

Cornbread is a Southern classic, known for its slightly sweet and buttery taste. It's a versatile bread that pairs perfectly with chili, stews, or as a side dish.

Directions

1. Preheat the oven and grease a baking dish.
2. In a bowl, mix cornmeal, flour, sugar, baking powder, and salt.
3. In another bowl, whisk together egg, milk, and vegetable oil.
4. Combine wet and dry ingredients.
5. Pour the batter into the baking dish.
6. Bake until golden brown.
7. Enjoy this classic and buttery cornbread.

Fun Fact

Cornbread is a Southern staple, perfect for those who savor the slightly sweet and buttery taste of this versatile bread, whether as a side or with hearty dishes.

12 muffins

160 calories per muffin

45 minutes

Cranberry Orange Muffins

Ingredients:

- 200g all-purpose flour
- 150g sugar
- 1 egg
- 80ml vegetable oil
- 120ml orange juice
- 5g baking powder
- 2g salt
- 150g dried cranberries
- Zest of 1 orange

Cranberry Orange Muffins are a burst of citrusy delight with the tartness of cranberries and the zest of oranges. They are a cheerful and fruity morning treat.

Directions

1. Preheat the oven and line a muffin tin with paper liners.
2. In a bowl, mix sugar, egg, vegetable oil, orange juice, and orange zest.
3. In another bowl, whisk together flour, baking powder, salt, and dried cranberries.
4. Combine wet and dry ingredients.
5. Fill each muffin cup 2/3 full.
6. Bake until golden brown.
7. Enjoy these citrusy and tangy muffins.

Fun Fact

Cranberry Orange Muffins are a zesty and fruity morning delight, perfect for those who relish the combination of cranberries and orange zest in a muffin.

1 loaf

180 calories per serving

60 minutes

Carrot Zucchini Bread

Ingredients:

- 200g all-purpose flour
- 150g sugar
- 2 eggs
- 120ml vegetable oil
- 5g baking powder
- 5g baking soda
- 2g salt
- 150g grated carrots
- 150g grated zucchini
- 5g cinnamon
- 50g chopped walnuts

Carrot Zucchini Bread is a moist and veggie-packed bread, combining the goodness of carrots and zucchini. It's a delightful way to enjoy your vegetables in a sweet treat.

Directions

1. Preheat the oven and grease a loaf pan.
2. In a bowl, mix sugar, eggs, and vegetable oil.
3. In another bowl, whisk together flour, baking powder, baking soda, salt, and cinnamon.
4. Combine wet and dry ingredients, then fold in grated carrots, grated zucchini, and chopped walnuts.
5. Transfer the batter to the loaf pan.
6. Bake until a toothpick comes out clean.
7. Enjoy this moist and veggie-infused bread.

Fun Fact

Carrot Zucchini Bread is a clever way to enjoy your veggies in a sweet and moist bread, perfect for those who love carrots and zucchini.

12 muffins

160 calories per muffin

40 minutes

Pumpkin Spice Muffins

Ingredients:

- 200g all-purpose flour
- 150g sugar
- 2 eggs
- 80ml vegetable oil
- 120ml canned pumpkin
- 5g baking powder
- 2g salt
- 2g ground cinnamon
- 1g ground nutmeg
- 1g ground cloves
- 1g ground ginger

Pumpkin Spice Muffins are a warm and spiced delight, filled with the flavors of autumn. They are a cozy and comforting morning indulgence or anytime treat.

Directions

1. Preheat the oven and line a muffin tin with paper liners.
2. In a bowl, mix sugar, eggs, vegetable oil, canned pumpkin, and spices.
3. In another bowl, whisk together flour, baking powder, and salt.
4. Combine wet and dry ingredients.
5. Fill each muffin cup 2/3 full.
6. Bake until golden brown.
7. Enjoy these spiced and cozy muffins.

Fun Fact

Pumpkin Spice Muffins are a warm and comforting treat, perfect for those who want to savor the flavors of autumn in a muffin.

1 loaf

190 calories per serving

60 minutes

Apple Cinnamon Bread

Apple Cinnamon Bread is a fragrant and fruity bread, showcasing the combination of apples and cinnamon. It's a delightful and cozy choice for any time of day.

Ingredients:

- 200g all-purpose flour
- 150g sugar
- 2 eggs
- 120ml vegetable oil
- 2 apples, peeled and diced
- 5g baking powder
- 5g baking soda
- 2g salt
- 5g ground cinnamon

Directions

1. Preheat the oven and grease a loaf pan.
2. In a bowl, mix sugar, eggs, and vegetable oil.
3. In another bowl, whisk together flour, baking powder, baking soda, salt, and ground cinnamon.
4. Combine wet and dry ingredients, then fold in diced apples.
5. Transfer the batter to the loaf pan.
6. Bake until a toothpick comes out clean.
7. Enjoy this fragrant and fruity bread.

Fun Fact

Apple Cinnamon Bread is a delightful and cozy choice for those who appreciate the sweet and spicy combination of apples and cinnamon in their bread.

9
squares

200
calories
per
serving

45
minutes

Cheddar Bacon Cornbread

Ingredients:

- 150g cornmeal
- 150g all-purpose flour
- 150g cheddar cheese, grated
- 100g cooked bacon, crumbled
- 5g sugar
- 5g baking powder
- 2g salt
- 1 egg
- 250ml milk
- 60ml vegetable oil

Cheddar Bacon Cornbread is a savory and cheesy delight, with the smoky goodness of bacon. It's a perfect side dish for soups, stews, or as a snack.

Directions

1. Preheat the oven and grease a baking dish.
2. In a bowl, mix cornmeal, flour, sugar, baking powder, and salt.
3. In another bowl, combine cheddar cheese, crumbled bacon, egg, milk, and vegetable oil.
4. Combine wet and dry ingredients.
5. Pour the batter into the baking dish.
6. Bake until golden brown.
7. Enjoy this savory and cheesy cornbread.

Fun Fact

Cheddar Bacon Cornbread is a smoky and cheesy delight, perfect for those who crave the rich taste of cheddar and bacon in their cornbread.

1 loaf

220 calories per serving

70 minutes

Chocolate Chip Pumpkin Bread

Ingredients:

- 200g all-purpose flour
- 150g sugar
- 2 eggs
- 120ml canned pumpkin
- 60ml vegetable oil
- 5g baking powder
- 5g baking soda
- 2g salt
- 150g chocolate chips

Chocolate Chip Pumpkin Bread is a delightful blend of pumpkin and chocolate chips, creating a sweet and moist bread. It's a perfect treat for those with a sweet tooth.

Directions

1. Preheat the oven and grease a loaf pan.
2. In a bowl, mix sugar, eggs, canned pumpkin, and vegetable oil.
3. In another bowl, whisk together flour, baking powder, baking soda, and salt.
4. Combine wet and dry ingredients, then fold in chocolate chips.
5. Transfer the batter to the loaf pan.
6. Bake until a toothpick comes out clean.
7. Enjoy this sweet and chocolatey bread.

Fun Fact

Chocolate Chip Pumpkin Bread is a sweet and indulgent treat, perfect for those who enjoy the combination of pumpkin and chocolate chips in their bread.

Chapter 10:
Bread for Special Diets

1 loaf

120 calories per serving

60 minutes

Keto-Friendly Almond Flour Bread

Ingredients:

- 200g almond flour
- 5g baking powder
- 2g salt
- 4 eggs
- 60ml olive oil
- 30ml almond milk

Keto-Friendly Almond Flour Bread is a low-carb delight, perfect for those following a ketogenic diet. It's a savory and nutty bread with a tender crumb.

Directions

1. Preheat the oven and grease a loaf pan.
2. In a bowl, whisk together almond flour, baking powder, and salt.
3. In another bowl, beat eggs, olive oil, and almond milk.
4. Combine wet and dry ingredients.
5. Transfer the batter to the loaf pan.
6. Bake until golden brown.
7. Enjoy this keto-friendly and nutty bread.

Fun Fact

Keto-Friendly Almond Flour Bread is a low-carb and savory choice, perfect for those on a ketogenic diet looking for a bread with a tender crumb.

1 loaf

150
calories
per
serving

50
minutes

Paleo-Friendly Coconut Bread

Paleo-Friendly Coconut Bread is a grain-free delight, suitable for those following a paleo diet. It's a moist and tropical-flavored bread with a hint of sweetness.

Ingredients:

- 200g coconut flour
- 5g baking powder
- 2g salt
- 4 eggs
- 60ml coconut oil
- 30ml honey
- 120ml coconut milk

Directions

1. Preheat the oven and grease a loaf pan.
2. In a bowl, combine coconut flour, baking powder, and salt.
3. In another bowl, beat eggs, coconut oil, honey, and coconut milk.
4. Combine wet and dry ingredients.
5. Transfer the batter to the loaf pan.
6. Bake until golden brown.
7. Enjoy this paleo-friendly and tropical bread.

Fun Fact

Paleo-Friendly Coconut Bread is a grain-free and tropical choice, perfect for those following a paleo diet and craving a hint of sweetness in their bread.

1 loaf

160 calories per serving

90 minutes

Vegan Whole Wheat Bread

Ingredients:

- 300g whole wheat flour
- 10g active dry yeast
- 5g sugar
- 5g salt
- 300ml warm water
- 30ml vegetable oil

Fun Fact

Vegan Whole Wheat Bread is a plant-based and hearty choice, perfect for those following a vegan diet and seeking a wholesome bread without dairy or eggs.

Vegan Whole Wheat Bread is a plant-based delight, suitable for those following a vegan diet. It's a hearty and nutty bread made without dairy or eggs.

Directions

1. In a bowl, dissolve yeast in warm water and let it proof with sugar.
2. In a large bowl, mix whole wheat flour and salt.
3. Stir in proofed yeast mixture and vegetable oil.
4. Knead the dough until smooth.
5. Let the dough rise until doubled in size.
6. Shape the dough into a loaf.
7. Let it rise again.
8. Preheat the oven and bake until golden brown.
9. Enjoy this vegan and nutty bread.

1 loaf

100 calories per serving

60 minutes

Low-Carb Cauliflower Bread

Ingredients:

- 300g cauliflower florets, steamed and riced
- 4 eggs
- 50g almond flour
- 5g baking powder
- 2g salt
- 5g garlic powder
- 5g dried oregano
- 5g dried basil

Low-Carb Cauliflower Bread is a creative and low-carb option, suitable for those looking to reduce their carbohydrate intake. It's a light and versatile bread.

Directions

1. Preheat the oven and grease a loaf pan.
2. In a bowl, mix steamed and riced cauliflower, eggs, almond flour, baking powder, salt, garlic powder, dried oregano, and dried basil.
3. Transfer the mixture to the loaf pan.
4. Bake until set and golden.
5. Enjoy this low-carb and creative bread.

Fun Fact

Low-Carb Cauliflower Bread is a creative and light choice, perfect for those seeking a low-carb option for their sandwiches and snacks.

1 loaf

140 calories per serving

90 minutes

Gluten-Free Chia Seed Bread

Ingredients:

- 300g gluten-free flour blend
- 10g active dry yeast
- 50g chia seeds
- 5g sugar
- 5g salt
- 300ml warm water
- 30ml olive oil

Gluten-Free Chia Seed Bread is a gluten-free delight, suitable for those with gluten sensitivities. It's a seedy and fiber-rich bread made without wheat.

Directions

1. In a bowl, dissolve yeast in warm water and let it proof with sugar.
2. In a large bowl, mix gluten-free flour blend, chia seeds, and salt.
3. Stir in proofed yeast mixture and olive oil.
4. Knead the dough until smooth.
5. Let the dough rise until doubled in size.
6. Shape the dough into a loaf.
7. Let it rise again.
8. Preheat the oven and bake until golden brown.
9. Enjoy this gluten-free and seedy bread.

Fun Fact

Gluten-Free Chia Seed Bread is a gluten-free and fiber-rich choice, perfect for those with gluten sensitivities looking for a bread packed with nutritious chia seeds.

1 loaf

140 calories per serving

70 minutes

Nut-Free Sunflower Seed Bread

Ingredients:

- 200g sunflower seed meal
- 50g flaxseed meal
- 5g baking powder
- 2g salt
- 4 eggs
- 60ml olive oil
- 120ml water

Nut-Free Sunflower Seed Bread is a safe and delicious option for those with nut allergies. It's a crunchy and flavorful bread made with sunflower seeds.

Directions

1. Preheat the oven and grease a loaf pan.
2. In a bowl, combine sunflower seed meal, flaxseed meal, baking powder, and salt.
3. In another bowl, whisk together eggs, olive oil, and water.
4. Combine wet and dry ingredients.
5. Transfer the batter to the loaf pan.
6. Bake until golden and set.
7. Enjoy this nut-free and crunchy bread.

Fun Fact

Nut-Free Sunflower Seed Bread is a safe and crunchy choice, perfect for those with nut allergies who want to enjoy a flavorful bread made with sunflower seeds.

1 loaf

110
calories
per
serving

80
minutes

Diabetic-Friendly Quinoa Bread

Diabetic-Friendly Quinoa Bread is a suitable option for those managing diabetes. It's a nutritious and low-glycemic bread made with quinoa flour.

Ingredients:

- 200g quinoa flour
- 50g flaxseed meal
- 5g baking powder
- 2g salt
- 4 eggs
- 60ml olive oil
- 120ml water

Directions

1. Preheat the oven and grease a loaf pan.
2. In a bowl, mix quinoa flour, flaxseed meal, baking powder, and salt.
3. In another bowl, beat eggs, olive oil, and water.
4. Combine wet and dry ingredients.
5. Transfer the batter to the loaf pan.
6. Bake until golden and set.
7. Enjoy this diabetic-friendly and nutritious bread.

Fun Fact

Diabetic-Friendly Quinoa Bread is a nutritious and low-glycemic choice, perfect for those managing diabetes and looking for a bread made with quinoa flour.

1 loaf

160 calories per serving

70 minutes

Dairy-Free Oat Bread

Dairy-Free Oat Bread is a lactose-free and hearty option for those with dairy allergies. It's a wholesome and oaty bread made without milk or butter.

Ingredients:

- 200g oat flour
- 50g flaxseed meal
- 5g baking powder
- 2g salt
- 4 eggs
- 60ml olive oil
- 120ml almond milk

Directions

1. Preheat the oven and grease a loaf pan.
2. In a bowl, combine oat flour, flaxseed meal, baking powder, and salt.
3. In another bowl, beat eggs, olive oil, and almond milk.
4. Combine wet and dry ingredients.
5. Transfer the batter to the loaf pan.
6. Bake until golden and set.
7. Enjoy this dairy-free and hearty bread.

Fun Fact

Dairy-Free Oat Bread is a lactose-free and hearty choice, perfect for those with dairy allergies and seeking a wholesome bread made without milk or butter.

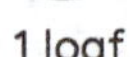

1 loaf

130
calories
per
serving

80
minutes

Approved Sweet Potato Bread

Ingredients:

- 200g sweet potato puree
- 100g almond flour
- 50g coconut flour
- 5g baking soda
- 2g salt
- 4 eggs
- 60ml olive oil
- 30ml coconut milk

Approved Sweet Potato Bread is compliant with the Whole30 program. It's a savory and satisfying bread made with sweet potatoes and approved ingredients.

Directions

1. Preheat the oven and grease a loaf pan.
2. In a bowl, mix sweet potato puree, almond flour, coconut flour, baking soda, and salt.
3. In another bowl, beat eggs, olive oil, and coconut milk.
4. Combine wet and dry ingredients.
5. Transfer the batter to the loaf pan.
6. Bake until golden and set.
7. Enjoy thisapproved and satisfying bread.

Fun Fact

Approved Sweet Potato Bread is compliant with the Whole30 program, making it a savory and satisfying option for those on this dietary plan.

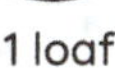

1 loaf

150 calories per serving

90 minutes

Sourdough Spelt Bread (Low FODMAP)

Ingredients:

- 300g spelt flour
- 10g sourdough starter
- 5g salt
- 300ml water

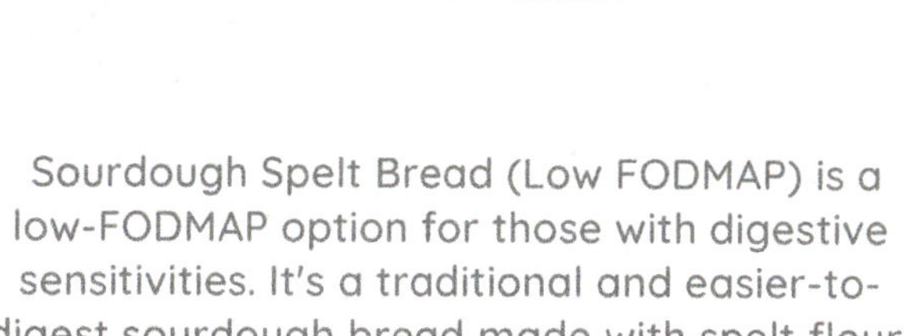

Sourdough Spelt Bread (Low FODMAP) is a low-FODMAP option for those with digestive sensitivities. It's a traditional and easier-to-digest sourdough bread made with spelt flour.

Directions

1. In a bowl, mix spelt flour, sourdough starter, salt, and water.
2. Knead the dough until smooth.
3. Let the dough rise until doubled in size.
4. Shape the dough into a loaf.
5. Let it rise again.
6. Preheat the oven and bake until golden and crusty.
7. Enjoy this low-FODMAP and traditional sourdough bread.

Fun Fact

Sourdough Spelt Bread (Low FODMAP) is a traditional and low-FODMAP choice, perfect for those with digestive sensitivities who want to enjoy sourdough made with spelt flour.

Chapter 11:
Breads
Beyond the
Basics

1 loaf

200 calories per serving

75 minutes

Garlic and Herb Monkey Bread

Garlic and Herb Monkey Bread is a savory and fun bread with aromatic garlic and fresh herbs. It's perfect for sharing with friends and family.

Ingredients:

- 300g all-purpose flour
- 5g sugar
- 5g salt
- 10g active dry yeast
- 240ml warm milk
- 30ml olive oil
- 5 cloves garlic, minced
- 15g fresh herbs (e.g., rosemary, thyme, parsley), finely chopped
- 60g butter, melted

Directions

1. Preheat the oven and grease a bundt pan.
2. In a bowl, mix flour, sugar, salt, and yeast.
3. Add warm milk and olive oil, knead until a smooth dough forms.
4. Let the dough rise.
5. Roll the dough into small balls.
6. Mix minced garlic and chopped herbs with melted butter.
7. Dip each dough ball in the garlic-herb butter and arrange them in the bundt pan.
8. Let it rise again.
9. Bake until golden brown.
10. Enjoy this savory and shareable monkey bread.

Fun Fact

Garlic and Herb Monkey Bread is a fun and savory bread perfect for sharing, featuring aromatic garlic and fresh herbs, a crowd-pleaser for any occasion.

1 loaf

220 calories per serving

90 minutes

Stuffed Cheese and Onion Bread

Stuffed Cheese and Onion Bread is a cheesy and flavorful delight with a surprise inside. It's a perfect accompaniment to soups and salads.

Ingredients:

- 300g all-purpose flour
- 5g sugar
- 5g salt
- 10g active dry yeast
- 240ml warm milk
- 30ml olive oil
- 100g grated cheese (e.g., cheddar)
- 1 onion, finely chopped
- 60g butter, melted

Directions

1. Preheat the oven and grease a loaf pan.
2. In a bowl, mix flour, sugar, salt, and yeast.
3. Add warm milk and olive oil, knead until a smooth dough forms.
4. Let the dough rise.
5. Roll out the dough into a rectangle.
6. Spread melted butter, cheese, and chopped onion over the dough.
7. Roll up the dough, forming a loaf.
8. Place it in the loaf pan.
9. Let it rise again.
10. Bake until golden and cheese is bubbly.
11. Enjoy this cheesy and surprise-filled bread.

Fun Fact

Stuffed Cheese and Onion Bread is a flavorful and cheesy delight, perfect for those who appreciate the surprise of cheese and onion inside their bread.

1 loaf

230 calories per serving

120 minutes

Cranberry Walnut Braided Bread

Cranberry Walnut Braided Bread is a sweet and nutty bread with a beautiful braided design. It's a delightful addition to your holiday table.

Ingredients:

- 300g bread flour
- 5g sugar
- 5g salt
- 10g active dry yeast
- 240ml warm water
- 30ml olive oil
- 100g dried cranberries
- 100g chopped walnuts
- 1 egg, beaten for egg wash

Directions

1. Preheat the oven and line a baking sheet.
2. In a bowl, mix bread flour, sugar, salt, and yeast.
3. Add warm water and olive oil, knead until a smooth dough forms.
4. Let the dough rise.
5. Divide the dough into three equal portions and roll them into ropes.
6. Braid the ropes and form a loaf.
7. Let it rise again.
8. Brush with beaten egg.
9. Sprinkle cranberries and walnuts on top.
10. Bake until golden brown.
11. Enjoy this sweet and beautiful braided bread.

Fun Fact

Cranberry Walnut Braided Bread is a sweet and visually stunning addition to your table, featuring dried cranberries and chopped walnuts for a delightful flavor.

1 loaf

250
calories
per
serving

180
minutes

Chocolate Babka

Chocolate Babka is a decadent and twisted bread filled with rich chocolate swirls. It's a true indulgence for chocolate lovers and special occasions.

Ingredients:

- 300g all-purpose flour
- 60g sugar
- 5g salt
- 10g active dry yeast
- 240ml warm milk
- 60g butter, melted
- 100g dark chocolate, finely chopped
- 30g cocoa powder
- 60g sugar
- 10g ground cinnamon

Directions

1. Preheat the oven and grease a loaf pan.
2. In a bowl, mix flour, 60g sugar, salt, and yeast.
3. Add warm milk and melted butter, knead until a smooth dough forms.
4. Let the dough rise.
5. Roll out the dough into a rectangle.
6. Mix dark chocolate, cocoa powder, 60g sugar, and ground cinnamon.
7. Spread the chocolate mixture over the dough.
8. Roll up the dough and slice it in half lengthwise.
9. Twist the two halves together.
10. Place it in the loaf pan.
11. Let it rise again.
12. Bake until golden and chocolate is melted.
13. Enjoy this decadent and twisted babka.

Fun Fact

Chocolate Babka is a decadent and twisted bread, a true indulgence for chocolate lovers, perfect for special occasions when you want to treat yourself.

1 loaf

210 calories per serving

120 minutes

Fig and Anise Pull-Apart Bread

Fig and Anise Pull-Apart Bread is a sweet and aromatic bread with delightful pockets of fig and anise flavor. It's perfect for brunch or dessert.

Ingredients:

- 300g all-purpose flour
- 60g sugar
- 5g salt
- 10g active dry yeast
- 240ml warm milk
- 60g butter, melted
- 100g dried figs, chopped
- 10g ground anise

Directions

1. Preheat the oven and grease a loaf pan.
2. In a bowl, mix flour, 60g sugar, salt, and yeast.
3. Add warm milk and melted butter, knead until a smooth dough forms.
4. Let the dough rise.
5. Roll out the dough into a rectangle.
6. Spread dried figs and ground anise over the dough.
7. Roll up the dough and slice it into small pieces.
8. Arrange the pieces in the loaf pan.
9. Let it rise again.
10. Bake until golden and figs are soft.
11. Enjoy this sweet and aromatic pull-apart bread.

Fun Fact

Fig and Anise Pull-Apart Bread is a sweet and aromatic delight, perfect for brunch or dessert, with delightful pockets of fig and anise flavor that surprise your taste buds.

1 loaf

240 calories per serving

100 minutes

Sun-Dried Tomato and Olive Bread

Sun-Dried Tomato and Olive Bread is a Mediterranean-inspired delight with the rich flavors of sun-dried tomatoes and olives. Perfect for serving with dips.

Ingredients:

- 300g bread flour
- 10g sugar
- 5g salt
- 10g active dry yeast
- 240ml warm water
- 30ml olive oil
- 100g sun-dried tomatoes, chopped
- 100g black olives, pitted and chopped
- 5g dried oregano

Directions

1. Preheat the oven and grease a loaf pan.
2. In a bowl, mix flour, sugar, salt, and yeast.
3. Add warm water and olive oil, knead until a smooth dough forms.
4. Let the dough rise.
5. Incorporate sun-dried tomatoes, black olives, and dried oregano into the dough.
6. Shape the dough into a loaf.
7. Let it rise again.
8. Bake until golden brown.
9. Enjoy this Mediterranean-inspired bread.

Fun Fact

Sun-Dried Tomato and Olive Bread is a Mediterranean-inspired delight, with the rich flavors of sun-dried tomatoes and olives, perfect for dipping and savoring.

1 loaf

260 calories per serving

120 minutes

Caramelized Onion and Gruyere Bread

Caramelized Onion and Gruyere Bread is a savory masterpiece with the sweetness of caramelized onions and the richness of Gruyere cheese. Perfect for a cozy night.

Ingredients:

- 300g bread flour
- 10g sugar
- 5g salt
- 10g active dry yeast
- 240ml warm water
- 30ml olive oil
- 2 large onions, thinly sliced and caramelized
- 150g Gruyere cheese, grated
- 10g fresh thyme leaves

Directions

1. Preheat the oven and grease a loaf pan.
2. In a bowl, mix flour, sugar, salt, and yeast.
3. Add warm water and olive oil, knead until a smooth dough forms.
4. Let the dough rise.
5. Incorporate caramelized onions, grated Gruyere cheese, and fresh thyme into the dough.
6. Shape the dough into a loaf.
7. Let it rise again.
8. Bake until golden and cheese is bubbly.
9. Enjoy this savory and cozy bread.

Fun Fact

Caramelized Onion and Gruyere Bread is a savory masterpiece, combining the sweetness of caramelized onions and the richness of Gruyere cheese for a cozy and delightful experience.

1 loaf

230 calories per serving

110 minutes

Everything Bagel Bread

Everything Bagel Bread brings the beloved flavors of an everything bagel into a soft and aromatic loaf. It's perfect for breakfast or brunch.

Ingredients:

- 300g bread flour
- 10g sugar
- 5g salt
- 10g active dry yeast
- 240ml warm water
- 30ml olive oil
- 30g everything bagel seasoning mix
- 1 egg, beaten for egg wash

Directions

1. Preheat the oven and grease a loaf pan.
2. In a bowl, mix flour, sugar, salt, and yeast.
3. Add warm water and olive oil, knead until a smooth dough forms.
4. Let the dough rise.
5. Incorporate everything bagel seasoning mix into the dough.
6. Shape the dough into a loaf.
7. Let it rise again.
8. Brush with beaten egg and sprinkle more seasoning on top.
9. Bake until golden and aromatic.
10. Enjoy this everything bagel-inspired bread.

Fun Fact

Everything Bagel Bread brings the beloved flavors of an everything bagel into a soft and aromatic loaf, perfect for breakfast or brunch, making every bite taste like an everything bagel.

1 loaf

270 calories per serving

140 minutes

Bacon and Cheese Filled Bread

Bacon and Cheese Filled Bread is a savory indulgence with crispy bacon and melty cheese hidden inside. It's a treat for bacon and cheese enthusiasts.

Ingredients:

- 300g bread flour
- 10g sugar
- 5g salt
- 10g active dry yeast
- 240ml warm water
- 30ml olive oil
- 150g cooked bacon, crumbled
- 150g cheddar cheese, shredded

Directions

1. Preheat the oven and grease a loaf pan.
2. In a bowl, mix flour, sugar, salt, and yeast.
3. Add warm water and olive oil, knead until a smooth dough forms.
4. Let the dough rise.
5. Roll out the dough into a rectangle.
6. Sprinkle crumbled bacon and shredded cheddar cheese over the dough.
7. Roll up the dough and seal the edges.
8. Place it in the loaf pan.
9. Let it rise again.
10. Bake until golden and cheese is bubbly.
11. Enjoy this indulgent bacon and cheese-filled bread.

Fun Fact

Bacon and Cheese Filled Bread is a savory indulgence with the delightful surprise of crispy bacon and melty cheese, a treat for those who love bacon and cheese.

1 loaf

220 calories per serving

100 minutes

Pesto Swirl Bread

Ingredients:

- 300g bread flour
- 10g sugar
- 5g salt
- 10g active dry yeast
- 240ml warm water
- 30ml olive oil
- 100g basil pesto
- 5g grated Parmesan cheese

Pesto Swirl Bread is a vibrant and flavorful bread with the green goodness of pesto swirled throughout. It's a taste of Italy in every slice.

Directions

1. Preheat the oven and grease a loaf pan.
2. In a bowl, mix flour, sugar, salt, and yeast.
3. Add warm water and olive oil, knead until a smooth dough forms.
4. Let the dough rise.
5. Roll out the dough into a rectangle.
6. Spread basil pesto and grated Parmesan cheese over the dough.
7. Roll up the dough and seal the edges.
8. Place it in the loaf pan.
9. Let it rise again.
10. Bake until golden and aromatic.
11. Enjoy this vibrant and Italian-inspired bread.

Fun Fact

Pesto Swirl Bread is a vibrant and flavorful delight with the green goodness of pesto swirled throughout, offering a taste of Italy in every slice.

We have a small favor to ask

As we reach the final pages of our exploration into the world of bread baking with "Breads Baking Made Easy: Knead to Know - Uncover the Secrets of Effortless Baking with Our 100+ Recipes Pictures Included," I'd like to make a sincere request.

Reviews, my fellow bakers, are akin to the perfect rise in a well-crafted loaf—essential, elevating, and deeply valued. For a small publisher like us, they are the crucial yeast that helps our creative efforts flourish.

If you could spare a moment, I kindly ask you to return to the platform where you discovered this baking treasure—whether it's an app or an online marketplace. There, much like the finishing touch of a perfectly scored crust, you'll find the review button. We would be truly grateful if you could share your honest rating and a brief, thoughtful sentence encapsulating your baking journey.

Every review is a pinch of salt for us, the element that makes our cookbook truly flavorful, and they mean more to us than the perfect crumb structure in a well-baked bread. In the spirit of transparency, should you encounter a minor hiccup within these pages, please know that we've kneaded and proofed our best efforts into this collection. We're not infallible, and, much like the occasional uneven rise, small mistakes can happen. We hope you can appreciate the overall baking experience despite these minor imperfections.

Your support, conveyed through a review, is like the perfect balance of ingredients in a masterfully crafted dough—it completes the experience and inspires us to keep sharing the secrets of effortless baking. So, if you can find the time, let your words be the extra dusting of flour on our baking masterpiece.

We deeply appreciate your time, your discerning taste, and your dedication to the art of bread baking. After all, this cookbook isn't just about recipes; it's about empowering you with the knowledge to knead with confidence. With heartfelt gratitude, we eagerly await your feedback. May your future baking endeavors be as satisfying and enriching as the ones in our cookbook.